SELF CONTROL AND ANGER MANAGEMENT LESSONS FOR MIDDLE AND HIGH SCHOOL STUDENTS

Activity Guide and Student Materials

GERRY DUNNE, Ph.D.

Copyright © 2019, Innerchoice Publishing • All Rights Reserved.

Student Experience Sheets may be reproduced in quantities sufficient for distribution to students in programs utilizing **SELF CONTROL AND ANGER MANAGEMENT LESSONS FOR MIDDLE AND HIGH SCHOOL STUDENTS**. All other reproduction, in any manner or for any purpose whatsoever, is explicitly prohibited without written permission. Request for such permission should be directed to INNERCHOICE PUBLISHING.

ISBN - 10: 1-56499-099-0

ISBN - 13: 978-1-56499-099-0

INNERCHOICE Publishing
15079 Oak Chase Court
Wellington, FL 33414

www.InnerchoicePublishing.com

To inquire regarding presentations and classes led by the author contact:

Gerry Dunne, Ph.D.: (360) 666-5057

gerrydunne1023@gmail.com

Printed in the United States of America.

If ever there was a stage of life when self control and anger management should be learned, it would be the teen years.

Many thanks to the coaches and contributors to this project

who generously gave their ideas and support,

especially:

Dennis Alberson, LCSW

Janis Aull, LCSW

Susanna Palomares, President, Innerchoice Publishing

and

Marilyn Firth, Editor Extraordinaire

CONTENTS

INTRODUCTION	1
Tips for Teaching the Lessons	3
Ideas for the Student Experience Sheets	5
The Ground Rules	6
Lesson 1: It's Just a Feeling!	9
Lesson 2: What's Under that Volcano?	17
Lesson 3: You Be the Judge!	24
Lesson 4: What about the Consequences?	33
Lesson 5: Look at It Another Way	37
Lesson 6: How Do You Talk to Yourself?	45
Lesson 7: Avoid these Four Traps!	51
Lesson 8: Four More Traps to Avoid!	60
Lesson 9: Grudges are Poison	69
Lesson 10: Revenge Is Not Sweet for Long!	75
Lesson 11: Start Out Fresh!	82

Lesson 12: Use Your Anger—Don't Let It Use You!   87

Lesson 13: You've Got the Power!   93

Lesson 14: Be Assertive!   100

Lesson 15: Stand Up For Yourself!   109

Lesson 16: Assertive Conflict Management Strategies that Work!   116

Lesson 17: More Assertive Conflict Management Strategies that Work!   124

Lesson 18: Don't Cave to the Pressure!   132

Lesson 19: How to Respond to Bullying Behavior   137

Lesson 20: Check Your Memory!   143

Introduction

If I'd participated in lessons like the ones in this manual when I was the age of your students I know I would have lived a healthier and happier life. I was one of those youngsters who grew up in a family that denied not only the importance of feelings but usually feelings themselves, especially uncomfortable ones. Yet, our feelings are the prime movers of our choices and actions.

Looking back I recall that just about everyone in my family and at school frequently lived in a state of unrest. They had axes to grind—things to complain about. They were annoyed! Sometimes they were hateful and harsh with their words. Yet from the outside everyone thought our family was about as normal and good as a family could get. All of us did, in fact, love each other. We just put our anger first too many times. My junior high and senior high schools were also considered normal, "a cut-above" actually, but I remember very little joy and a lot of fear, hurt and shame.

I realize now how much I was influenced by this general discontent and pervasive anger. I grew up assuming that spreading gossip, fighting, holding grudges, protesting anything I didn't like and planning ways to get even were just what you did! Life wasn't normal unless you had a good, strong aggravation going about something or someone.

Did you have similar experiences? Are your students caught up in this kind of world? Some people are lucky. They're born into, and surrounded by, great circumstances and great models. But many others aren't. The fact is that many of us have, or had, anger habits that started early in our lives—habits we didn't even know we had. Inevitably, this means few skills in self control and anger management will develop. The result: troubles and misery as life unfolds.

If you'd told me a few decades ago that I had an anger habit I would have either denied it or said, "No big deal—so what? Who doesn't?" But that kind of blindness wasn't working very well for me. At a certain point I realized it and started to make some deliberate changes.

I still struggle with my own anger at times but I've also recognized it for what it is. I became more self-honest. I've been working on understanding how anger operates and developing skills to use *it* instead of letting it control and use *me*. I took courses in psychology and wound up with a Ph.D. in Developmental Psychology which focuses on how people are affected by their experiences as they navigate through each stage of life. I went to some helpful counselors and I read a lot of excellent books. For the last ten years I've taught Anger and Conflict Management at Clark College in Vancouver, Washington using the text, *Anger and Conflict Management: Personal Handbook*.

Developing self control and learning how to manage anger leads us out of a dark world into a new one we've lit up ourselves. It's a world with healthy relationships, fun, more friends and enjoyment—also some detachment when it comes to difficult situations. I'm living in that world most of the time now *and I seek more company.*

I wrote this manual with its 20 lessons specifically to help you lead your students through a learning process that can place them on the road to Positive Personal Power!

Gerry Dunne

Tips for Teaching the Lessons

Emphasize student participation. The lessons in this guide are largely experiential and interactive, encouraging student involvement and input. The lessons include class discussions, pairings, teams, role playing and dramatization. The experience sheets offer opportunities for reading, journaling, and taking quizzes. When students engage in these types of learning experiences they will likely find the ideas and strategies for self control and anger management interesting and worthwhile. Since students themselves are the primary resource, physical preparations are neither elaborate nor expensive.

Since the subject matter can be emotionally sensitive and students in this developmental stage are generally self conscious, the lessons have been carefully structured to reduce confusion and embarrassment as much as possible. Examples: students are asked to verbally share only what would be comfortable for them to share. They are also asked not to name names when discussing their observations of other people's behavior. The ground rules offered in this introductory section will also help the students understand how important it is for them to behave respectfully toward one another as they engage in the lessons.

It would be ideal if the class is well trained in team projects, group discussions, and "pair and share" activities but if they are not this is a good time to help them become accustomed to interacting with peers in the classroom by assigning these types of activities for academic lessons.

Teach the lessons in their presentation sequence. The lessons have been developed in a sequence that gradually builds from understanding the value of self control and anger management to practicing assertive and constructive anger management strategies. There are also certain sequences that are particularly closely scaffolded--best taught in the sequence offered such as Lessons three, four and five. Lessons seven and eight which are actually parts one and two of the same lesson, are another example. And lessons 14, 15, 16 and 17 are another prime example. Each lesson has, however, been developed as a "stand alone" learning activity. Beyond these "rules of thumb," as all teachers know, it can be fruitful to insert a lesson when the need for its focus has become apparent.

Allow time to complete each lesson. Each lesson has been designed to be completed within one class period. Group size and other factors may extend or shorten the sessions.

Utilize the Student Experience Sheets. The ideas, concepts and skills offered in this curriculum may seem deceptively simple but they are not easy for many people to employ in everyday life. The experience sheets provide repetition of these important themes and their various reiterations in order for students to more thoroughly align their own thinking and actions accordingly. Research has shown the value of repetition for helping students gain understanding and internalization of these kinds of concepts as well as commitment to using the skills in their everyday lives.

Use your own words. Suggestions are offered for what to say to the students at strategic points in each lesson. These *italicized* statements are clearly shown with quotation marks. Reading these statements aloud to the students during the lesson is not recommended, however, because doing so tends to yield a "flat" presentation. It is best to read them to yourself before the lesson. Then make each of the statements in your own words when you teach the lesson.

Form teams and pairings using your own judgement. You know your students—who works well with whom, who should not be paired with whom, and other considerations regarding your social and physical environments. However, here are some rules of thumb: (1) The best number of students per team is four. (2) Keep teams and pairings intact for a number of meetings then rearrange them. (3) Immediately shift combinations if an unforeseen difficulty between students arises.

Roles for team members are suggested for some of the lessons which may be useful for your class. These roles include: discussion leader, reader, recorder and reporter.

Put yourself into it! Don't hesitate to augment the curriculum with your own creativity as all good teachers do. Give your own dramatic flair to explanations of concepts. Play a video with a relevant example or a popular song that exemplifies the ideas and concepts of a particular lesson. And to the extent that you are comfortable doing it, share anecdotes from your own life that illustrate key points in the lessons

Ideas for the Student Experience Sheets

The titles of the Student Experience Sheets are the same as the titles of the lessons they accompany. As noted above, they provide repetition of the key ideas and concepts as well as team, partner, and individual activities. In some cases these activities are integral to the lessons and in other cases they supplement the lessons. The first few experience sheets are given to the students at the end of the lessons for personal review and to introduce the kinds of ideas and suggestions that future experience sheets will offer.

Suggestion: provide folders or binders for the students for collecting their completed experience sheets. At times they may wish to refer to former experience sheets as they work on a current one. This practice will be especially helpful for the twentieth lesson: "Check Your Memory" if you choose to make the test "open book."

Another idea: Lesson 20, "Check Your Memory" could be used as a pre-post test. If you choose this option it is likely that the students will correctly fill in some of the blanks on the pre-test. Make it clear, however, that you do not expect them to be able to figure them all out. It will, no doubt, be interesting after the post-test when you have taught all of the lessons to compare the two sets of scores and even challenge the students to perform the math to show their learning gains.

The Ground Rules

The ground rules are particularly important when teams of four (and pairings) work together. Your expectation that the students honor the ground rules is essential to the success of the lessons. It is recommended that the ground rules be presented to the students and discussed before lesson one begins and at strategic times thereafter as necessary. It is also recommended that the ground rules be posted in a prominent place in the classroom.

An additional recommendation: give students who will not cooperate or behave in a disruptive manner individualized, alternative assignments.

GROUND RULES FOR PARTICIPATING IN SELF CONTROL AND ANGER MANAGEMENT LESSONS

1. Everyone is welcome to speak during class and in small group discussions to share feelings and opinions, and to ask questions.

2. We will share only those personal experiences we feel comfortable sharing.

3. No one will ever be forced to speak. Listening is a contribution.

4. We will always listen to the person who is speaking.

5. We will do our best to share speaking times equally.

6. We will not interrupt, pry, or put each other down in any way.

7. We will not gossip (no naming names) in class or outside of class.

Everyone is affected by many types and degrees of anger--our own and the anger of others. It is a powerful emotion and a sensitive subject. Anger deserves our attention, investigation, respect and careful handling.

In class we will foster:

- Safety
- Respect
- Dignity
- Understanding
- Empathy
- Support
- Friendship
- Laughter and Enjoyment

We will avoid:

- Gossip
- Put downs
- Uncomfortable confessions
- Prying
- Blaming
- Ranting
- Guilt

Lesson 1: It's Just a Feeling!

Purpose:

This opening activity helps students understand:

- Anger is simply one of many normal human emotions, and as such, is neither good nor bad in a moral sense. (It's just a feeling.)
- Everyone has the right to feel anger when provoked.
- The feeling of anger can range from mild irritation to outrage and fury.
- Anger can spur behavior that is unproductive and destructive or productive and constructive. The feeling and the behavior are two different things.
- People differ in what provokes them to feel anger and the degree of anger they feel is different for different people.
- Anger can be managed through self control.
- Self control is the secret to personal power.

Materials:

A copy of the Student Experience Sheet #1, "It's Just a Feeling!" for each student; Four post-its for every student

Preparations:

Before beginning this lesson which calls for teams to share ideas and personal stories, present and discuss the Ground Rules for Participating in Self Control and Anger Management Lessons with the students (see page 6). It is also recommended that these ground rules be posted in a prominent place in the classroom.

Write the slogans provided in Step 13 on a whiteboard or flipchart. Hide them from view.

Directions:

1. **Motivate the students to develop Personal Power!** Tell the class in your own words: "*Today we are going to begin some lessons about developing the most awesome power a person can have: personal power! This power is an achievement that results from self-control.*

"Gaining this power is a major challenge and the best time to start making it happen in our lives is right now! Why is it a major challenge? Because it's so easy to lose control of ourselves when we become angry especially when the anger is intense. Yet anger is nothing more than a normal feeling all of us experience from time to time just like all the other feelings we experience.

"Let's start by taking a good look at anger so we can understand it better. That's the first step in learning how to manage it and gain personal power!"

2. **Begin with a class anger list.** Write, **What makes you angry?** at the top of a blank whiteboard or chart. Then ask the class to contribute to a list of things that anger them. Respectfully chart their statements. Add your own contribution to the list as well.

3. **Rank the student's anger statements.** After a list of around ten statements have been charted ask the contributors to rate their degrees of anger in relation to their statements. Use ratings of 1 through 5. (Five is angriest possible; 1 is mild irritation; levels 2, 3, and 4 are the levels in between.) Write the number each student states next to his or her statement.

4. **Explain how we are the same and different:** *"Yes, anger happens to us all! There are lots of things on this list that make me mad too but I would rank some of them with a different number. Did you notice that too? Does that mean someone is wrong if we have different levels of anger for the same things? No. All it means is that we are just naturally different from each other in what angers us and the degree to which we feel it."*

5. **Acknowledge how powerful anger can be.** Ask, *"What does anger feel like? If it were a thing what would it be—a rhinoceros on the charge, a bomb going off? What image comes up for you?"* (Tip: if no one mentions a volcano, mention it yourself.)

6. **Pose the key question: *Is anger bad?*** *"I have a question for you to answer in your head, just to yourself. ... Is anger bad?"* Give the students some time to ponder the question.

7. **Explain this key concept:** *"Many people have bad feelings about themselves when they feel angry or just afterward. They do their best to avoid anger or deny it when it happens. But anger is not bad--or good; it's just a feeling. Guilt, embarrassment, and shame are unhelpful feelings about your own anger. The fact is that you feel what you feel. Accepting your anger, which takes self-honesty, is the first step in taking charge of it. WHAT YOU DO WITH YOUR ANGER IS WHAT MATTERS!"*

8. **Describe self control and anger management:** *"As we have discussed, anger is a very powerful emotion and all of us know that when anger is acted on in destructive ways people can get hurt. Feelings and actions are not the same thing. Self control is feeling something that might lead you to a destructive action but you take hold of yourself and you don't allow yourself to do it. That's anger management! The fact is that anger can even be acted on constructively when you are really in control of yourself."*

9. **Share a brief personal story.** Tell the class about a time you would be comfortable sharing when you responded to a provoking situation in a constructive manner and how you felt about yourself afterwards.

10. **Form teams of four. Topic: "A Time I Used Self Control."** Elaborate on the topic: *"Bring to mind a situation you are proud of. If you wish to take a turn to speak to your team members, describe a time when you became angry and handled yourself well so that you didn't get hurt in any way and no one else did either. This might have even been a time when the result was better for everyone involved. Describe your feelings, what you thought to yourself, what you did, and how things turned out."*

11. **Give the signal to begin.** *"Make sure everyone on your team who wants to speak has a chance to do so. Save questions for each other until everyone who wishes to speak has had a turn. You have _____ minutes. One more thing: if you decide to speak be sure it's something you would feel comfortable sharing. Go."*

12. **Guide a follow-up discussion with the entire class.** Ask:

    — *"Could you relate to any of the situations you heard your team members tell about? How so?"*

    — *"Could you relate to the feelings other students on your team felt? How so?"*

    — *"Did you hear some good ideas for managing anger? Let's hear some examples."*

13. **Reveal the slogans you previously wrote on the whiteboard and hid from view.** Conduct a group reading of the slogans out loud.

> *Anger Happens!*
>
> *Anger—it's just a feeling!*
>
> *Anger can be managed!*
>
> *Feelings and actions are two different things.*
>
> *Self-control = Personal Power!*
>
> *Anger is felt differently by different people!*
>
> *I don't have to hurt someone or myself when I'm angry.*
>
> *Don't let anger cause you to mess up!*

14. **Distribute the post-its for writing slogans.** Give 16 post-its to each team of four so that each student will have four. Refer to the slogans on the whiteboard. Suggest: *"Write the four slogans you like best on the post-its. Stick them on yourselves or on a book—anywhere. Take them home and stick them where you will see them. They can be a handy reminder to help you understand other people and yourself better when anger happens. They can also help you remember to stay in control of yourself and manage your anger."*

    Ask the students if they can come up with other slogans that sum up what they learned. Write them on the whiteboard. (Respectfully reject any that miss the mark.) If the students request additional post-its for writing more slogans provide them.

    Display your own set of post-its with the slogans for the rest of the day on your clothing or some other obvious place.

15. **Initiate another time for team members to talk with each other.** Topic: "Why I Chose These Four Slogans." Provide sufficient time for the teams to share why the slogans they chose are the most meaningful to them. (This topic might be altered to "The Slogan I Like Best," if time is short.)

16. **Distribute Student Experience Sheet #1, "It's Just a Feeling."** Ask the students to read all of it and then to fill in their personal responses to the questions by themselves.

17. **Explain the purpose of the experience sheet:** *"This experience sheet provides a review of what we've been focusing on. It's a way to help you learn these important ideas through repetition. What you write is personal; it's just for you to use to help you become more self controlling and to gain personal power."*

It's Just a Feeling!

Student Experience Sheet #1

What makes you angry? Make a list:

_____ _____
_____ _____
_____ _____
_____ _____
_____ _____
_____ _____
_____ _____
_____ _____

Rate your degrees of anger. Write a 5 by the things that make you the most angry (furious, outraged) and a 1 by things that mildly irritate you. Four, 3, and 2 are the levels in between.

If anger was a thing what would you call it and why"

_____
_____
_____
_____
_____
_____
_____

Is anger bad?

Think about this: Many people have bad feelings about themselves when they feel angry or just afterward. They do their best to avoid anger or deny it when it happens. But anger happens! It's not bad--or good; it's just a feeling. Guilt, embarrassment, and shame are unhelpful feelings about your own anger. The fact is that you feel what you feel. Accepting your anger, which takes self-honesty, is the first step in taking charge of it.

WHAT YOU DO WITH YOUR ANGER IS WHAT MATTERS!

Did you know...?

- Anger is simply one of many normal human emotions, and as such, is neither good nor bad in a moral sense. ***(It's just a feeling.)***
- Everyone has the right to feel anger when provoked. That includes you. (It also includes people who may be mad at you!)
- The feeling of anger can range from mild irritation to outrage and fury.
- Anger can spur behavior that is unproductive and destructive or productive and constructive. The feeling and the behavior are two different things.
- People differ in what provokes them to feel anger and the degree of anger they feel is different for different people.
- Anger can be managed through self control.

Self control is the secret to personal power!

Recall a time when you managed your anger well—a time when nobody got hurt feelings or hurt physically. Describe it here:

_____
_____
_____
_____

Gaining personal power by being in control of yourself can be a huge challenge! Many people work on it their entire lives. Those who have it are respected by others. Who do you know, or know of, who fits this description? Write some notes to yourself about how this person acts when stressed or angry.

_____
_____
_____
_____
_____
_____

On the next page are some slogans to remember about anger— how to think about it and what to do with it. Read through the slogans and see if you can think of others?
Write them here:

_____
_____
_____
_____
_____
_____

This experience sheet is just for you to help you remember the ideas in Lesson One. You may share what you've written with others only if you wish to. Other experience sheets will be useful as your teacher or counselor offers more lessons on anger management and self control.

The goal: your confidence in yourself to continually gain positive personal power!

ANGER Happens!

Anger... It's just a FEELING!

Feelings and actions ARE TWO DIFFERENT THINGS.

ANGER CAN BE MANAGED!

❉ ◆ ❉ ◆ ❉ ◆ ❉

Anger is felt differently by different people!

Self-Control = PERSONAL POWER!

I don't have to hurt someone or myself when I'm ANGRY.

DON'T LET ANGER CAUSE YOU TO MESS UP!

Lesson 2: What's Under that Volcano?

Purpose:

This learning activity helps students understand:

- Anger is frequently a secondary emotion coming from the primary emotions of fear, hurt, anxiety, disappointment, frustration, distress, or grief. Often the unmanaged expression of these kinds of anger causes more fear, hurt, anxiety, disappointment, frustration, distress, or grief.

- Without conscious intent, people often change their sensitive underlying emotions, like fear or hurt, into anger because anger substitutes feelings of vulnerability with an emotion that seems to feel more powerful. The anger also distracts people from their real underlying feelings which are uncomfortable.

- Self-honesty is the first step in anger management. It allows people to avoid being victims to their own distorted anger and the destructive acting out and/or depression that can come from it.

- Unless people face into their real, underlying feelings with courage, it is unlikely that they will be able to resolve those feelings and choose the best ways to act.

Materials:

A copy of the Student Experience Sheet #2, "What's Under that Volcano?" for each student

Preparations:

Draw the picture to the right, including the lines, on a whiteboard or flipchart and hide it from view.

Directions:

1. **Motivate the students to examine anger.** Tell the class: *"Today we are going to explore anger together again and learn more about how it operates. In our last lesson we learned that it's just a feeling, a normal emotion just like all the others. However, anger has some unusual characteristics that make it hard to manage. It can be complex and tricky. So let's continue to look at it closely. The more we learn about it, the more we can become self-controlling and gain personal power."*

2. **Form pairs to discuss the dark side of anger.** As soon as the students are facing their partners, explain: *"Take turns telling each other about a time you saw someone in person or perhaps in a video or a movie in a very angry state, a time when their anger seemed overblown for the situation. In fact their anger seemed way beyond what you would have felt, and not only that, the person wasn't managing his or her anger but was behaving stupidly and destructively. It's important if it was an actual person you saw that you do not name him or her. Perhaps you could call the person, 'the human.' Just describe what you saw and how you felt about it. You have _____ minutes. Be sure you each get a turn. Go."*

3. **Reveal the drawing of the volcano.** Ask the students: *"A lot of the people you described to each other blew like this volcano, right?"* (Pause for their assent.) *"What do you know about volcanoes? What actually causes them to erupt?"*

   Discuss the fact that volcanoes erupt when the magma below the surface becomes so hot and pressured that it has no other place to go than up and out.

4. **Ask the first set of key questions:**

   — *"Now we come to the complex and tricky part of anger. How are people's angry eruptions and the eruptions of volcanoes alike?"* (Point to the line at the base of your volcano and the area below the line.)

   — *"What is down here underneath the surface in a person that causes anger and destructive acting out? Are there some more sensitive emotions underneath?"*

5. **Chart the underlying emotions named by the students on the vertical lines under the horizontal line at the base of the volcano.** To start the process, begin the list yourself, perhaps with the word, FEAR. (See example.) Tell the students about a time you would feel comfortable sharing when you became frightened and then the feeling changed into anger.

6. **Ask, Has anything like that ever happened to you?"** Add: *"If you choose to respond be sure it's something you'd be comfortable telling us about."* Listen to a few examples. Then proceed to write the words on the vertical lines below the volcano that describe the kinds of feelings the students reported that converted to anger and caused eruptions. The list could include:

FEAR	**HURT**	**ANXIETY**	**EMBARRASSMENT**
STRESS	**SADNESS**	**GRIEF**	**DISAPPOINTMENT**
FRUSTRATION			

   If students offer words like "aggravation" or "rage" write them on the vertical lines above the volcano because they describe the angry behavior that comes out. Ask for more versions of anger and write them above the volcano. Examples: "fury," "mad," and "annoyed."

7. **Discuss how and why underlying emotions cause eruptions:** Ask, *"Now, let's see if we can figure out why these underlying emotions change into anger?"* Through questioning and discussion help the students understand that: *"Without realizing it, we sometimes change more sensitive, underlying emotions like fear and hurt, into anger because anger gives us a more powerful feeling. No one likes to experience fear or hurt or any of the other sensitive underlying emotions. They make us feel vulnerable and miserable so we convert them into anger and pay attention to the anger instead of the first feeling."*

8. **Direct the students to return to their partners.** Challenge them: *"You have _____ minutes to help each other figure out what the underlying emotions might have been in the angry 'humans' you described to each other."*

9. **Challenge the class to identify the specific underlying emotions in the people they described to their partners.** Ask the class: *"Let's name some of the underlying emotions that you think may have caused the anger in the 'human' you told your partner about."*

10. **As each feeling is named underline it on the whiteboard where it is written under the volcano or add it if it was not stated before.** If time permits you might ask for a few of the stories they shared with their partners reminding them not to name the persons their stories were about.

11. **Increase the student's awareness of how anger operates.** Ask: *"How does it help us manage our anger and become more self-controlling if we know that sometimes our anger distracts us from a deeper, underlying emotion that's uncomfortable?"*

12. Discuss these final points with the students:

— *Self-honesty is the first step in anger management and personal power. This can be very difficult at times. It takes courage!*

— *When you are straight with yourself about what you are feeling, and face into those feelings with courage, you improve your position to make good judgements about how to help yourself.*

— *Sometimes asking for help sorting out your feelings with someone else you trust is the best thing to do.*

— *When you ignore or try to hide your feelings from yourself two damaging things can happen: going out of control and blowing like the volcano which can hurt or even destroy your relationships, or allowing the volcano to go off inside you which could cause you to become depressed.*

13. Distribute Student Experience Sheet #2, "What's Under that Volcano?" Direct the students to individually read all of it and to write their responses to the questions in the time remaining. Explain: *"Doing this provides some repetition of the main ideas in today's discussion about what sometimes lies beneath our anger and why it's best to be honest with ourselves about it."*

What's Under that Volcano?

Student Experience Sheet #2

Can you remember times when you've seen people "blow their tops" like a volcano going off? Pick one time and write about it in the space below.

It's okay if it was a person in a video or a movie. If it was a person you saw in life, don't name him or her. Instead, call the person, "the human."

_____
_____
_____
_____
_____
_____
_____
_____

By acting this way did this "human" gain your respect? _____

What was your reaction to this "human's" behavior:

_____
_____
_____
_____

21

On the illustration below write some words on the lines ABOVE the volcano showing what came out of it—words stating what the angry human did (examples: shout, swear, pound on something, etc.) and words that would describe his or her level or type of anger (examples: aggravated, furious, irate, etc.).

Did you know...?

- Anger is frequently a secondary emotion coming from the primary emotions of fear, hurt, anxiety, disappointment, frustration, distress, or grief. Often the unmanaged expression of this kind of anger causes more fear, hurt, anxiety, disappointment, frustration, distress, or grief.

- Without conscious intent, people often change their sensitive underlying emotions, like fear or hurt, into anger because anger substitutes vulnerable feelings with an emotion that seems to feel more powerful. The anger also distracts people from their real underlying feelings which are uncomfortable.

- Self-honesty is the first step in anger management. It allows people to avoid being victims to their own distorted anger and the destructive acting out and/or depression that can come from it.

- Unless people face into their real, underlying feelings with courage, it is unlikely that they will be able to resolve those feelings and choose the best ways to act.

Think back to "the human" again whose behavior you just described. Think about what made him or her erupt. What words would describe how he or she might have been feeling underneath the surface? Write them on the lines BELOW the illustration of the volcano.

Tips:

- You are a human too. Like all normal humans you can also feel anger that comes from deeper, uncomfortable emotions.

- Sometimes it can be very hard to honestly tell yourself the truth—how you are really feeling. But when you do it you help yourself make good decisions about what to do, and not do, so nobody gets hurt in any way, including you!

Lesson 3: You Be the Judge!

Purpose:

This learning activity helps students understand:
- Anger often occurs after deeper, primary emotions are felt. This kind of anger is often "blind," impulsively spurring behavior that is destructive to self and others.
- Instead of taking impulsive, destructive actions in provoking situations, it is possible to use judgement and decide to act in alternate ways that are constructive, or at least neutral.
- The key is the word, "decide!"

Materials:

A copy of the Student Experience Sheet #3, "You Be the Judge," for each student; a copy of one scenario (of eight provided) per team.

Preparations:

Copy all eight scenarios and cut them into separate scenarios so that each team will have a different one. Ask the teams to select one member to keep their copy for the next lesson.

Write the word, JUDGEMENT, on the whiteboard.

Note:

Step 2 gives directions for dividing the class into eight teams. This is the ideal grouping because eight scenarios are offered and all eight should be addressed for maximum benefit. The ideal number of students per team is four. Thus, if you have 32 students each of the eight teams will have four members. Make adjustments in the number of students per team that come as close to this ideal as possible. (If your group is small and there is sufficient time, each team may read and discuss more than one scenario. Another alternative for small groups is to cover four scenarios on one day and the other four on another day.)

Directions:

1. **Gain the student's attention by pointing to the word, JUDGEMENT.** Ask them what the word means to them. Listen to several responses. Then explain: *"You may not have thought of this before, but you are a judge! Many times every day each of us uses judgement again and again: what to wear, what to eat, what to say to someone, and so forth. But often we could use good judgement and forget to. The point of the activity we are about to do is to see where judgement fits into anger management and to become better judges of provoking situations and what to do in those situations."*

2. **Explain the procedure for forming teams:** *"We are going to divide the class into ___ teams of ____ members per team. I'll give each team a sheet of paper describing a scenario—something that has happened in the life of a student. It also has some ways the student could act in the situation. Your team's job will be to choose the best action and to explain to the class why it's best."*

3. **Challenge the teams to assign roles for each member.** After the teams are formed tell the students: *"Let's determine roles. Select a **reader** who will read your scenario and the four choices for action out loud to the team. Next, you will need a **discussion leader** who will make sure everyone who wishes to speak gets a chance. Third, you will need a **recorder** to take notes about the judgement your team reaches and why you chose it. Last, you will need a **reporter** who will read your scenario to the class and tell us what your team judged to be the best action and why. You have one half minute to determine roles. Any questions?"*

4. **Distribute one of the eight scenarios to each team.** Allow sufficient time for the teams to discuss their scenarios including the choices and questions offered. Serve as a consultant only when a team requests clarification saying as little as possible. These are judgements for the students to make. Encourage them to state their opinions on why their choice is best and to come up with other choices that might work. (The next lesson will allow them to focus on the likely consequences of the poor choices.)

5. **Facilitate the teams' reports.** Taking each team in turn direct the reporter to read his or her scenario to the class including all of the alternative actions offered. The reporter should tell which alternative his or her team thought was best and why. If his or her team came up with another constructive alternative the reporter should tell the class about it as well. (If a team jokingly reports an obvious poor choice laugh along with them. Then redirect them to choose again.)

6. **Distribute the Student Experience Sheet #3, "You Be the Judge!"** In the time remaining direct the students to read and discuss within their teams the seven scenarios their team didn't discuss previously as well as the "Did you know..." segment at the end. (It's identical to the purpose statement at the beginning of this lesson.)

7. **Thank the teams for stating their opinions and brainstorming possibilities.** Remind them: *"You can decide to make good judgements to manage your own anger 'in real life!'"*

Scenarios:

#1: Kelly and Mr. Donavan

Kelly is a very energetic student. A rule that is hard for him to follow is walking in the halls. He prefers to run as fast as he can. More than once he has knocked someone down. When this happens he is embarrassed but takes off if he can. One day a teacher, Mr. Donavan, catches Kelly sprinting down the hall for the third time in one week. He stops him and tells him to go with him to the office to see the vice-principal. Kelly is scared because teachers have taken him to the office too many times already for the same reason. Suddenly he becomes furious.

You be the judge! Kelly should:

1. Realize he's guilty of breaking a rule he has broken many times and apologize.
2. Tell Mr. Donavan in a loud voice that he didn't hurt anybody and having to go to the office isn't fair.
3. Clam up while giving Mr. Donavan and everyone in the office the meanest look he can put on his face.
4. Cut loose and run away.

#2: Angie and Teresa

Angie is having fun at a birthday party. She came with her friend, Teresa, who suddenly points at her and starts to laugh. Loudly Teresa tells everyone, "Hey look at Angie! What an airhead! She's got her shirt on inside out and backwards!" Angie is hurt and embarrassed. She turns red. Then she becomes angry.

You be the judge! Angie should:

1. Rush to the bathroom and not come back out until the party is over.
2. Scream at Teresa, "You witch! Look who's talking. A few days ago you wore one green sock and one blue sock to school."
3. Remain quiet and breathe deeply until she gets control of herself. Then she should smile and say, "Oh thanks, Teresa. I was wondering when someone would notice. I like this side of my shirt better."
4. Remain quiet and try to hide her embarrassment and anger from everyone including herself.

#3: Shelly and Jamal

Even before they were born Shelly and Jamal's families lived next door to each other and they have been friends. All this changed, however, when Jamal's dad got a transfer at work making it necessary for their family to move across the country. Even before Jamal moved away Shelly became sad and even sadder after he was gone even though they texted each other almost every day. Then Shelly got angry. One evening just before dinner her mom asked her to get her books and papers off the table where she had begun doing her homework. Shelly screamed, threw a book on the floor, and ran out of the room crying.

You be the judge! Shelly should:

1. Stay in her room the rest of the evening and not answer her family if they ask her to eat with them or try to talk with her.

2. Call Jamal long distance and yell at him for moving away.

3. Go outside and throw rocks at the garage.

4. Cry out her sadness, then return to the kitchen, pick up her books and papers, and tell her mom she's sorry for the way she acted. Then she might ask her mom (or someone else) if they could talk later about how she's been feeling since Jamal left.

#4: Harry

Last night Harry couldn't get to sleep because his parents were drinking and fighting. Again the next morning they were shouting at each other as he dressed and left for school. Harry is anxious that his parents won't be able to live with each other much longer. He doesn't know what will happen if they split up. It's all he can think about and he's becoming more and more depressed and irritable with his friends.

You be the judge! Harry should:

1. Bury his feelings about the situation and stay away from home as much as possible.

2. Talk with an adult he trusts about the situation, and his feelings, even if he might cry during their talk. He could also ask the adult if they could meet again whenever he was feeling really upset.

3. Interrupt his parents during their next fight by yelling at them and breaking things.

4. Pour all the liquor in the house down the drain and leave broken bottles all over the kitchen floor when his parents aren't home. Then take off.

#5: Brennan, Nicole and Enrique

Brennan and Nicole are "an item." They're in the same grade and live on the same block. Every afternoon after school they walk home together talking. Brennan asked Nicole to go to a game with him next week. Nicole said sure, of course. Then they met Enrique, a new boy who is two years older and very good looking. Brennan invited him to the game too. But Brennan was hurt, disappointed, and jealous when Nicole became friendly with Enrique and gave him more attention during the game than she gave him. Before the event was over Brennan became angry.

You be the judge! Brennan should:

1. Get up and walk out before the game is over.
2. Nudge Nicole and say, "Hey, what's wrong with you? How rude can you get?"
3. Join Nicole and Enrique's conversation. Be friendly and talk with other people seated nearby as well.
4. Decide to ignore his feelings and hope that Nicole will never act this way again.

— — — — — — — — — — — — — — — — — — — —

#6: Hunter

Hunter was very premature at birth. All his life he's had trouble focusing and has had memory problems. (This does not happen to every person who was premature at birth.) The best thing Hunter can think of to do when his problems cause him trouble is to make excuses. When he entered his math classroom and discovered that his teacher was handing out tests to the students he was shocked and got scared because he had not prepared for the test. He had completely forgotten about it. Suddenly Hunter was fuming with anger.

You be the judge! Hunter should:

1. Calm himself down by breathing deeply and reassuring himself that he knows enough to do fairly well on the test. Then he should take the test and do the best he can.
2. Tell the teacher in a loud voice—and falsely--that she had forgotten to remind them the day before about the test and that it isn't fair to make him take it.
3. Lie and say he's feeling sick and has to leave.
4. Punish himself by telling himself he's an idiot, and deserves to flunk the test.

#7: Brigitte and Billy

Billy is Brigitte's seven-year old brother. Frequently Brigitte discovers that Billy has come into her room and taken things. This causes her a lot of frustration. She has screamed at him to stop doing it. But now and then Billy just can't resist the temptation to enter Brigitte's room and "borrow" things. He also enjoys antagonizing her. One day Brigitte comes home from school to find Billy in the family room playing a CD she recently bought and put in one of her drawers. Brigitte is extremely upset.

You be the judge! Brigitte should:

1. Call Billy a thief and hit him.
2. Give up on the whole situation and go to her room in a fury saying nothing to Billy.
3. Say or do nothing until her dad comes home. Then she should tell her dad what happened demanding that he solve the problem.
4. Push the power button, remove the CD, and tell Billy in a strong, steady voice how angry she is. Later she could ask her dad to join her in a talk with Billy to help him understand that what he's been doing is not okay.

#8: Ramona

Ramona is always rushing and stressed because she has too many things going on at the same time. Besides school, she takes piano lessons, voice lessons, and has joined three different clubs. She also plays forward on the soccer team. Her parents have encouraged her but she agreed to all of these activities herself. One afternoon Ramona rushes into the gym to suit up for soccer practice and suddenly realizes she left her practice shoes and clothes at home. She's wearing a skirt and sandals. There's no way she can participate in practice wearing what she has on. Soccer is the activity she likes best. Ramona is very annoyed.

You be the judge! Ramona should:

1. Kick her locker door until she bends it.
2. Tell her parents to call the teachers and sponsors of her clubs to get her out of them.
3. Ask her teammates to loan her some practice shoes and clothes. Then burn off her anger in practice and, realizing that she is too stressed with too many activities, decide to drop some of them--but not soccer.
4. Go home and yell at her parents for making her get involved in so many activities.

You Be the Judge!

Student Experience Sheet #3

Your teacher or counselor will give you a scenario of something that happened in the life of a student causing him or her to become angry. Read and talk about the scenario with the members of your team.

You be the judge. Choose the action that you believe would be the best thing for the student to do. Then answer the questions about your choice and why it would work better than the other choices. See if you can come up with some other choices that might work well for the student.

Please keep your copy of the scenario. It will come in handy for the next lesson.

1. What is your role on your team? _____

2. What is the number of your team's scenario? # _____

3. What is the name of the student in your scenario? _____
_____

As you give your opinion and listen to your team members write notes here that you believe are important to keep in mind:

_____
_____
_____
_____

Write down the number of the action that shows the most careful judgement and self-control? #_____

Why is it best?

_____
_____
_____
_____
_____
_____

What other choices might work well for the student?

_____
_____
_____
_____
_____
_____

Did you know ...?

- Anger often occurs after deeper, primary emotions are felt. This kind of anger is often "blind" impulsively spurring behavior that is destructive to yourself and others.

- Instead of taking impulsive, destructive actions in provoking situations, it is possible to use judgement and decide to act in other ways so that no one gets hurt especially you!

- The key is the word, "decide!"

Remember! You can decide to make good judgements to manage your own anger "in real life!"

Lesson 4: What about the Consequences?

Purpose:

This learning activity helps students understand:

- Impulsive actions taken without using judgement and self-control can lead to unpleasant and unrewarding consequences not only for themselves but others too.
- It is smart to consider the consequences of an action before doing it especially when they are angry.
- Considering consequences of an action before doing it is an important element in self control and anger management and a great way to develop personal power.

Materials:

A copy of the Student Experience Sheet #4, "What about the Consequences?" for each student; a copy of the same scenario the teams discussed for Lesson 3 for each team

Preparations:

Write the word, CONSEQUENCES, on the whiteboard.

Notes:

Plan to divide the class into the same teams as for Lesson 3. Each team will need a copy of the same scenario they discussed in Lesson 3.

This lesson emphasizes more to be learned from the scenarios presented in Lesson 3, You Be the Judge! It is designed to increase the student's awareness of how many ways things can go wrong when they allow themselves to take impulsive actions without considering the consequences.

Directions:

1. **Gain the student's attention by pointing to the word, CONSEQUENCES on the whiteboard and explaining the procedure.**
   First, briefly discuss the meaning of "consequences" with them. You might tell them a personal story you would be comfortable sharing about a time—perhaps when you were their age—when you took an impulsive action

without considering the consequences and the results, which you didn't see coming, were unfavorable.

Next, explain: *"Today we are going to discuss the same scenarios you talked about before in your teams with a different focus and with different roles. Your challenge is to brainstorm in more detail what you think might happen if the student in your scenario actually did the actions that were not best. In other words, what consequences might occur to him or her and to the other people in the scenario? You could even brainstorm what unfortunate fallout might occur to the student in your scenario and others beyond the immediate future. Chances are the poor choices could set things in motion over time causing even more trouble and pain for him or her."*

2. **Re-form the teams and direct the students to change roles:** *"**Choose a new leader, reader, recorder and reporter.** Your new reporter will tell the class what some of the consequences were for one of the poor choices that your team came up with. You have _____ minutes. Any questions?"*

3. **Distribute copies of the Student Experience Sheet #4 "What about the Consequences?" to all of the students.** Ask them to pick one poor choice for their report to the class. (Provide a new copy of the scenarios to the teams that did not retain their copies from Lesson 3.)

4. **Visit the teams.** As the teams discuss the consequences of the poor choices, pull up a chair and sit in on each discussion for a few minutes. Minimally join the discussions as you see fit.

5. **Facilitate the teams' reports to the class on the consequences they brainstormed.** Taking each team in turn, direct the reporter to reread aloud his or her team's scenario to the class including all of the alternative actions. The action judged best by the team should be repeated. Finally, ask the reporter to describe the short and long term consequences his or her team came up with for one of the poor choices.

6. **Refer the teams back to their experience sheets.** Direct the reader on each team to read the "Did you know..." segment to the team. Encourage them to discuss these points and possibly give examples from their own lives that they would be comfortable sharing.

7. **Thank the students for their good thinking and comments.** Point out: *"Learning the importance of considering the consequences of our actions is a lesson everyone needs to learn in life. When you learn this at your age you are at an advantage."*

What about the Consequences?

Student Experience Sheet #4

Did you know ...?

- Impulsive actions taken without using judgement and self-control can lead to unpleasant and unrewarding consequences not only for you but others too.
- It is smart to consider the consequences of an action before doing it especially when you are angry.
- Considering consequences of an action before doing it is an important element in self control and anger management and a great way to develop personal power.

With your team members, look back at the scenario you focused on in Lesson 3, "You Be the Judge." This time you will have the opportunity to brainstorm with your team members what might happen if the student impulsively acts on one of the poor choices.

1. What is your new role on your team? _____

2. What is the number of your team's scenario? _____

3. What is the name of the student in your scenario?
   _____

4. Write down the poor choice your team selects to brainstorm:
   _____
   _____
   _____

Use this space for listing the consequences your team brainstorms that might occur if the student impulsively acts on the poor choice your team selected. The consequences could be both short term and long term.

_____

_____

_____

_____

_____

_____

_____

_____

_____

Write notes here about the consequences the other teams brainstormed for their scenarios and reported to the class:

_____

_____

_____

_____

_____

_____

Learning the importance of considering the consequences of your actions is a lesson everyone needs to learn in life. Learning this when you are young places you at an advantage.

Lesson 5: Look at It Another Way

Purpose:

This learning activity helps students understand:

- Our senses—seeing, hearing, smelling, tasting and touching—form our perceptions.
- We interpret our perceptions into thoughts like conclusions and judgements, which in turn spur feelings and actions.
- Our interpretations of perceptions are based on past experiences.
- Different people interpret situations they perceive differently. This is because no two people have had the same past experiences.
- Sometimes our interpretations of perceptions lead to incorrect conclusions and judgements as well as inappropriate—even damaging--emotions and actions. These are called "distortions."
- It is helpful at times to ask ourselves if we can look at a situation another way instead of basing our conclusions, judgements, emotions and actions on what we think we are perceiving at first.
- Opening our minds to looking at situations in other ways helps us correct our own distortions and to feel genuine empathy for other people.

Materials:

A copy of Student Experience Sheet #5, "Look at It Another Way" for each student; a copy of the New Version Scenarios provided in this lesson of the same situation the teams discussed in Lessons 3 and 4 for each team.

Preparations:

Write the words, PERCEPTION, INTERPRETATION and DISTORTION on the whiteboard. Copy all eight New Version Scenarios. Cut them into separate scenarios and provide each team with its new version of the scenarios they discussed in Lessons 3 and 4.

Notes:

Plan to divide the class into the same teams as for lessons 3 and 4.

This lesson builds on what was learned in Lesson 3, "You Be the Judge!" and Lesson 4, "What about the Consequences?" It is designed to increase the student's awareness of, and respect for, the perceptions, thoughts and feelings of others in the circumstances and situations life offers.

Directions:

1. **Gain the student's attention by pointing to the words, PERCEPTION, INTERPRETATION and DISTORTION.** Briefly discuss their meanings with the students using the seven bulleted purpose points above.

2. **Explain the procedure for looking at the eight scenarios in another way:** *"Today we are going to discuss the scenarios you talked about before in your teams one more time with yet a different focus and with different roles. Your challenge, and it's a big one, is to look at the situation in the scenario your team has focused on from the point of view of another person in the scenario. Each of you should imagine you are that person and discuss together how that person might change his or her interpretation of what he or she perceived and how best to act based on looking at the situation in another way."*

3. **Reform teams and distribute copies of Student Experience Sheet #5, "Look at It Another Way"** and a copy of the new version of the same situations the teams discussed in Lessons 3 and 4 to each team. Direct the students to reassign themselves new roles. Ask the reader on each team to read the "Did you know..." segment to the team and the two paragraphs that follow it at the bottom of page 42, as well as the new version of their scenario. Finally, ask the teams' leaders to lead a discussion about how this new character could look at the situation another way. Circulate and serve as a consultant while the students hold their discussions. Give them as much latitude as possible.

4. **Facilitate the teams' reports on how the new characters in their scenarios could look at their situations in another way.** Taking each team in turn, direct the reader to reread his or her team's scenario on Student Experience Sheet #3, "You Be The Judge," to the class including all of the alternative actions. Additionally, the reader should read the new description on Student Experience Sheet #5, "Look at It Another Way" to the class. Finally, the reporter should tell the class how his or her team thought the new character could look at the situation another way and even adjust his or her actions.

5. **Direct the teams to gain a broader focus toward open mindedness and empathy.** Acknowledge that the behavior of some of the students, such as Shelley yelling at her mom and Hunter making excuses, is inappropriate but the reason to look at their situations differently wasn't to judge them. Rather, it was to be more understanding of them. Shelley was grieved and Hunter may have been disabled and troubled. In other cases of inappropriate behavior like Ramona's we can see how unfair she was to her dad and learn from her error.

6. **Close by directing the student's attention to the last paragraph on their experience sheets.** Ask a student to read it aloud.

New Version Scenarios

#1 Kelly and Mr. Donavan

Imagine that you are Mr. Donavan. You've seen Kelly run in the hall and even knock people over too many times. You are annoyed. You tell him he's going to the office to see the vice principal. But then Kelly comes clean and says, "Mr. Donavan, I admit I broke the rule again and I apologize. I promise to try my best not to do it again."

Mr. Donavan thinks to himself, "Kelly seems to be sincere." Then he asks himself, "Is there another way to look at this situation?"

- - - - - - - - - - - - - - - - -

#2 Angie and Teresa:

This time imagine you are Teresa. You just pointed out that Angie's shirt is inside out and backward. You think it's no big deal, just funny. But Angie has stopped talking. She won't look at you or anyone else. You're surprised that she's acting this way. You think, "She's no fun—can't take a joke."

But then, as Teresa, you remember how you felt when your brother told your boyfriend that you talk weird stuff in your sleep all the time. You ask yourself, "Is there another way to look at this situation?"

- - - - - - - - - - - - - - - - -

#3 Shelley and Jamal

Imagine that you are Shelley's mom. You are shocked and upset by Shelley's behavior which seems to have "come from nowhere." You feel like giving her a stern lecture.

As Shelley's mom, you wait before you do anything. After you calm down you ask yourself what's going on inside your daughter and you wonder what could be causing her emotions to be so raw. Then you wonder, "Is there another way to look at this situation?"

#4 Harry

Imagine that you are one of Harry's friends. You've heard he has it rough at home but you're getting tired of how irritable and depressed he's been lately. You feel like dropping him as a friend.

Then, as Harry's friend, you think about what he's going through and how tough it must be for him. You ask yourself, "Is there another way to look at this situation?

- - - - - - - - - - - - - - - - - - - -

#5 Brennan, Nicole and Enrique

Imagine that you are Nicole. You've been talking with Enrique at the game more than you've talked with your boyfriend, Brennan. You didn't mean to ignore Brennan and you are shocked when he starts criticizing you for it. He's annoyed and now so are you. Everybody goes quiet.

Then, as Nicole, you remember times when you felt ignored and left out. You ask yourself, "Is there another way to look at this situation?"

- - - - - - - - - - - - - - - - - - - -

#6 Hunter

Imagine that you are one of Hunter's classmates. You've known him for a long time. When you notice he obviously forgot about the math test and then says he's sick and has to leave you think, "There he goes again making excuses for not preparing for the test like I did." You feel like blurting out that he's a flake.

Then, as his classmate, you start to wonder why Hunter forgets things and makes excuses so often. You ask yourself, "Is there another way to look at this situation?"

- - - - - - - - - - - - - - - - - - - -

#7 Brigitte and Billy

Imagine that you are seven-year old, Billy. You've been telling yourself it's no big deal to sneak into Brigitte's room and take things. You think she's overreacting way too much when she gets so frustrated about it. Then your friend, Dylan, who's your same age tells you how mad he is at his little sister who keeps sneaking into his room and taking his things.

As Billy, this causes you to think about Brigitte's feelings and ask yourself, "Is there another way to look at this situation?"

8 Ramona

Imagine that you are Ramona's dad. You have encouraged her to participate in activities she enjoys. You always let her choose what she wants to do. Now Ramona is blaming you and her mom for making her get involved in too many activities. You are disappointed in her for being so unfair. You threaten that if she ever talks to you like that again you will put her on lock down for being so unreasonable and disrespectful.

As Ramona's dad you know you need to think about the situation so you go for a walk. You calm down and admit to yourself that you have involved yourself in too many activities in the past at times and that you didn't want to blame yourself for doing it. You ask yourself, "Is there another way to look at this situation?"

Look at It Another Way

Student Experience Sheet #5

Did you know ...?

- Our senses—seeing, hearing, smelling, tasting and touching—form our perceptions.
- We interpret our perceptions into thoughts like conclusions and judgements, which in turn spur feelings and actions.
- Our interpretations of perceptions are based on past experiences.
- Different people interpret situations they perceive differently. This is because no two people have had the same past experiences.
- Sometimes our interpretations of perceptions lead to incorrect conclusions and judgements as well as inappropriate—even damaging--emotions and actions. These are called "distortions."
- It is helpful at times to ask ourselves if we can look at a situation another way instead of basing our conclusions, judgements, emotions and actions on what we think we are perceiving at first.
- Opening our minds to looking at situations in other ways helps us correct our own distortions and to feel genuine empathy for other people.

Your teacher, or counselor, is going to give you a new version of the same scenario you've been focusing on with your team.

Now there is a new development! Something else happens in the scenario that might cause you to "see" things differently from the point of view of another person in the scenario. It could be something the person notices or realizes now that he or she didn't notice or realize before, or it could be some new action someone takes.

1. What is your new role on your team? _____

2. Who are you imagining you are now in the scenario? _____
   _____

3. Describe the new development that happens? _____
   _____
   _____
   _____
   _____
   _____
   _____

4. How does this new development affect your point of view now—as the person in the scenario that you are imagining you are?
   _____
   _____
   _____
   _____
   _____
   _____

5. What do you think would be the best action to take now—as the person in the scenario that you are imagining you are?
   _____
   _____
   _____
   _____
   _____
   _____

6. Is there a situation in your own life that might benefit you to look at it in another way? Write down how you could look at that situation differently and what you might say or do to make the situation better.

_____
_____
_____
_____
_____
_____
_____
_____
_____
_____
_____
_____

It's a challenge to examine your first reaction to a situation and then to look at it another way. To do this it might mean "stepping into the shoes" of other people and considering their feelings and point of view. It's an ability that leads to understanding and compassion with outcomes that are good for everyone. It's also another way to build personal power!

Lesson 6: How Do You Talk to Yourself?

Purpose:

This learning activity helps students understand:
- Thoughts are self-talk.
- Self-talk can be helpful and encouraging or hurtful and damaging.
- In upsetting situations helpful self-talk leads to self-control and anger management.
- Self-talk can be controlled and guided allowing you to calm yourself and think carefully about what's going on and what to do. That's personal power!

Materials:

A copy of Student Experience Sheet #6, "How Do You Talk to Yourself?" for each student

Directions:

1. **Gain the student's interest by asking, "How do you talk to yourself?"** After a pause to let the question "sink in," tell the class about an anger-provoking personal situation you would feel comfortable sharing in which you calmed and encouraged yourself with positive self-talk. (Examples: "I'm angry, but I can stay calm......, Chill out now......, R-e-l-a-x....., I can figure out what to do......., I can handle this...... .") It could be a recent event or one that occurred perhaps when you were the age of your students.

2. **Find out what the students noticed.** Ask: *"Did you notice what I did to help myself so that things would work out okay?"* Help them understand that your self-talk made all the difference. You "coached" yourself through some tough moments to keep your emotions and your thoughts steady leading to a good action.

3. **Focus on what the effects of negative self-talk might have been.** Ask the students, *"What could I have said to myself that would have set me up to lose control and act destructively?"* Listen to their responses.

4. **Challenge the students to remember the alternatives they thought were best.** Ask, *"Think back to the scenarios you examined in your teams in the prior three lessons. Can you remember some alternatives that you judged best that undoubtedly included positive self-talk?"*

5. **Clue the students how the characters might have used positive self talk:**

   #1 Kelly, when he was honest about his habit of running in the hall and apologized;

   #2—Angie, when she breathed deeply and stayed calm, then "thanked" Teresa;

   #3—Shelly, when she went to her room, cried, apologized, then realized she might have a heart-to-heart talk with her mom or someone else;

   #4—Harry, when he decided to talk with an adult he trusts;

   #5—Brennan, when he decided to join Nicole and Enrique's conversation and start new conversations with other people;

   #6—Hunter, when he calmed himself down and realized he knew enough to do fairly well on the math test;

   #7—Brigitte, when she told her little brother how his behavior made her feel and then arranged a serious discussion about it with their dad;

   #8—Ramona, when she decided to ask her teammates to loan her some practice clothes.

6. **Distribute the Student Experience Sheet #6, "How Do You Talk to Yourself?"** Tell the students: *"Let's read these situations that would likely upset most anyone and imagine that each one is happening to you. Then I'll give you a few minutes to write something positive and encouraging you could say to yourself in your mind for each situation on your experience sheet. What you write should be something to calm you and help you use your good judgement to respond in a reasonable way—to do something helpful for yourself and anyone else who might have been involved. Later, you will have a chance to share some of the positive 'self-talk' ideas you have written down with your team. Are you ready?"*

7. **Read aloud with the students the five descriptions of anger-provoking situations listed on the Experience Sheet.** Ask for first reactions from a few students for each one. Make this fun. Explain, *"Often our first reactions to situations like these produce unhelpful self talk. That's okay. You can always calm yourself down and correct negative self talk with helpful self talk once you realize what you are doing to yourself."*

8. **Provide an appropriate amount of time for the students to write down their thoughts for each of the anger-provoking situations on their experience sheets.**

9. **Form teams of four to discuss how positive self talk could help them.** Explain: *"Take about _____ minutes to share some of the ideas you wrote down about what you could say to yourself that would be helpful when you are in anger-provoking situations like these. Make sure everyone on your team who wants to have a turn gets a chance. Go for it."*

10. **Read and discuss the "Let's review..." segment at the end of the experience sheet with the class.** (It's identical to the purpose statement at the beginning of this lesson.) Be sure to discuss the final tip about the value of taking deep breaths when stressed.

11. **Close with this challenge: Be your own coach!** *"For the rest of the day, see how many times you can be in total charge of yourself by guiding your own thoughts in ways that calm you when something upsetting happens. In fact, be your own coach tomorrow too—and into the future! When you do this you can take deserved pride in your "mental smarts" and your actions that give you personal power!"*

How Do You Talk to Yourself?

Student Experience Sheet #6

It happens to all of us so often. We forget things. We say the wrong thing when we really wanted to say the right thing. We stumble. We hiccup. People laugh at us. You name it. Often our first reaction to situations like these produces unhelpful self talk. We blame ourselves or somebody else. We feel embarrassed and apologize too much or we clam up thinking that if we say something it will be stupid. All of that is just being human and it's okay. Always remember, you CAN calm yourself down and correct negative self talk with helpful self talk. You can be your own coach!

Here are some situations that can be anger-provoking for almost anyone. Write down some ideas for things you could say to yourself that could calm you down and help you figure out what to do that would be helpful.

- You get to school and discover that you forgot your homework.

_____

_____

_____

- You tell a friend something that you need to talk about and ask her not to tell anyone else. Two days later another student comes up to you and asks you about it. It's obvious that your friend told other people.

_____
_____
_____
_____

- You have to give an oral report in class and the other students know that you would rather not. They are smirking at you and rolling their eyes as you begin.

_____
_____
_____
_____

- You trip in the hall and fall down. A guy you thought was your friend, laughs and calls you a dork.

_____
_____
_____
_____

- Your hair won't do what you want it to.

_____
_____
_____
_____

Now think of a situation that may or will occur sometime soon that you aren't looking forward to. Perhaps you've been thinking some negative thoughts about it. See how well you can program yourself with positive self talk to help yourself with it. Write down what you might start saying to yourself here:

_____
_____
_____
_____
_____
_____
_____
_____
_____
_____
_____

Let's review...
- Thoughts are self-talk.
- Self-talk can be helpful and encouraging or hurtful and damaging.
- In upsetting situations helpful self-talk leads to self-control and anger management.
- Self-talk can be controlled and guided allowing you to calm yourself and think carefully about what's going on and what to do. That's personal power!

Tip! Double the strength of positive self talk by taking deep breaths when you are stressed. Bring the air in through your nose and breathe out through your mouth.

Lesson 7: Avoid these Four Traps!

Purpose:

This learning activity helps students understand:
- Certain typical mental and emotional "snares" or "traps" make it difficult for people to make good choices, stay in control of themselves, and manage their anger.
- It is easiest to avoid these traps when you know about them.
- The four traps to avoid are: "past/present mixups," "gunnysacking," "acting on habit," and "having unrealistic expectations." Each one usually leads to unpleasant consequences.
- **Past and present mixups** happen when people think the same painful past event is happening again causing them the same painful upset as before. In truth, no two events are exactly the same—only similar.
- **Gunnysacking** is putting up with many upsetting situations over a short time period ("stuffing the gunnysack") without resolving or solving them in some way. Then, when one more irritation occurs the "gunnysacker" angrily erupts.
- **Acting on habit** is the "programmed" way people react to annoyances. They behave the same way every time.
- When a person has **unrealistic expectations** for something that is not realistically obtainable they set themselves up for disappointment and put an unfair strain on others who are expected to deliver what was expected.

Materials:

A copy of Student Experience Sheet #7, "Avoid these Four Traps!" for each student

Preparations:

Draw the diagram on the next page on the whiteboard or chart for the students to see as they enter the classroom. (Feel free to add your own "artistic touches" to the figure.)

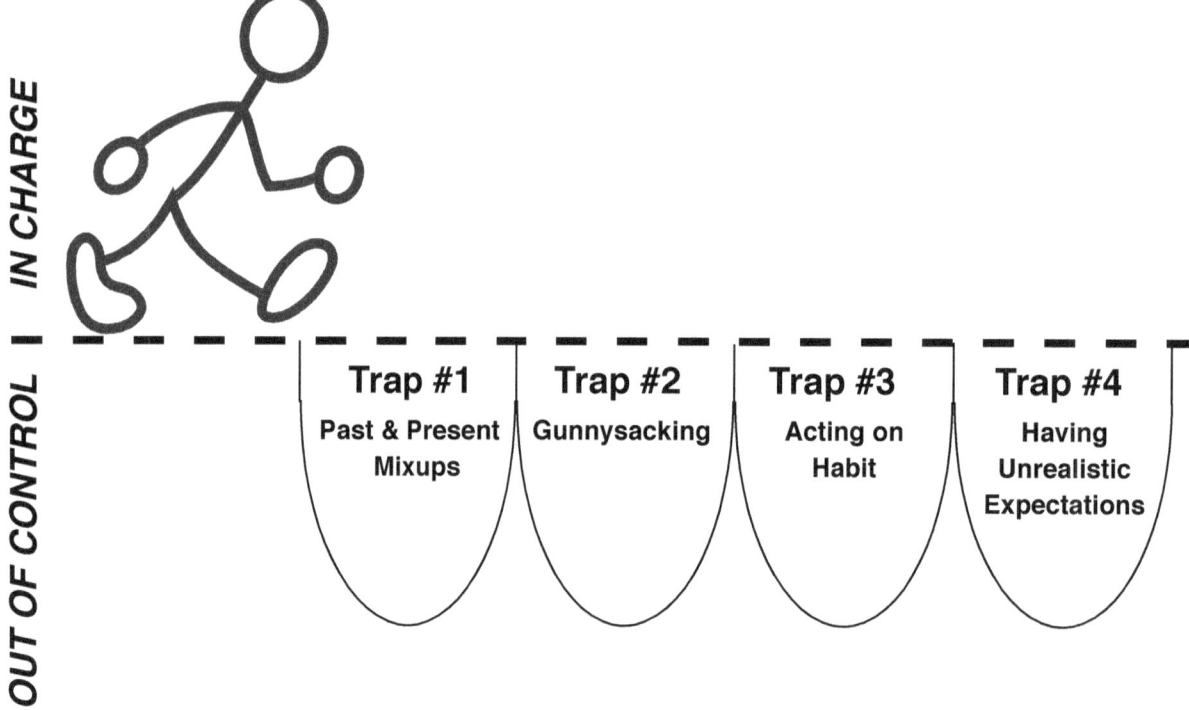

Note:

The next lesson, "Four More Traps to Avoid!" naturally follows this one.

Directions:

1. **Intrigue the students by asking, *Have you fallen into a trap lately?"*** Elaborate: *"We have been learning about how to control ourselves and manage our anger when we get mad. Today let's get realistic and talk about why self-control can be hard at times. (Point to the drawing on the whiteboard.) Tell the students, "When you are operating above this line, you are in charge of yourself because you are staying out of these traps even when provoking things happen and you feel anger. As soon as you let your anger cause you to fall into one of the traps below the line, you may not realize it, but you have lost control of yourself. The result could likely be some very unpleasant consequences for you and possibly others. Let's find out what these traps are."*

2. **Form Pairs to discuss the traps.** As soon as the students are facing their partners, explain: *"I'm going to name and describe each of these traps. After I describe each one you will have ____ minutes to talk with your partner about it. Maybe you recognize that you have fallen into it or you saw it happen to somebody else. If you talk about other people please don't mention their names. Any questions?"*

3. **As you describe each trap draw a line that dips into it.**

4. **Point to Trap #1, "Past & Present Mixups."** Describe it: *"This is probably the most common of all the traps. People can frequently get upset if something happens in the present that reminds them in some way of something bad that happened in the past. For example: someone unfairly criticizes you in front of other people and you become angry for good reason. From then on, however, your anger comes back and you get a bad feeling when someone even mentions the name of the person who unfairly criticized you. The name is no more than a word and a sound made in present time, yet you get a negative feeling inside as if the person was standing there and the episode was happening again."*

5. **Direct the students to talk with their partners about "past and present mixups" for two minutes.** Start them off with, *"Has something like this ever happened to you or have you seen it happen to someone else?"* (Remind them to tell their partners only stories they would feel comfortable sharing and not to name names.)

6. **Point to Trap #2, "Gunnysacking."** Describe it: *"Have you ever put up with bothersome things over and over again? Then suddenly it happens once more--the last straw--which makes you blow like a volcano and completely lose control of yourself? This trap is very common. It happens because we just keep collecting these irritations and frustrations instead of dealing with them or resolving them in some acceptable way. Then the load gets to be too much. This trap is called 'gunnysacking' because we keep filling up our imaginary gunnysack with things that make us mad. Then, when it gets to be too much we GO mad."*

7. **Direct the students to talk with their partners about "gunnysacking."** Start them off with, *"Has something like this ever happened to you or have you seen it happen to someone else?"*

8. **Point to Trap #3, "Acting on Habit."** Describe it: *"You have probably noticed how some people become angry in the same way in the same kinds of situations again and again. They 'act on habit' as if they were robots. It's much easier to see in others than to recognize in ourselves, but the chances are that you have some anger habits too. Think about it: are there any sorts of situations that consistently upset you and you just act the same way whenever these situations occur? It's as if your button gets pushed and you go into motion without stopping to think things over and maybe decide to act differently. Sometimes other people catch on to your 'buttons' or 'anger triggers' and enjoy pushing your button or pulling your trigger just to watch you go into your noisy routine. Does this sound familiar?"*

9. **Direct the students to talk with their partners about "acting on habit."** Start them off with, *"Has something like this ever happened to you or have you seen it happen to someone else?"*

10. **Point to Trap #4, "Unrealistic Expectations."** Describe it: *"This is the last trap and another easy one to fall into. Have you ever been angry because you didn't get something you really wanted? Of course. It's happened to us all, but sometimes the thing we set our minds on is not realistically attainable and we just don't want to admit that to ourselves. We set ourselves up for disappointment and our anger is actually bogus when our expectations are unrealistic. Not only that, we place unfair blame on whoever was supposed to deliver the goods. You have, no doubt, seen this happen with others? Can you be honest with yourself and recognize that maybe you have done it too?"*

11. **Direct the students to talk with their partners about "unrealistic expectations."** Start them off with, *"Has something like this ever happened to you or have you seen it happen to someone else?"*

12. **Tell the students that in the next lesson four more traps will be revealed.** Ask if they can think what those traps might be. Listen to their responses but, to build some suspense, don't give anything away.

13. **Ask, "How is it helpful to know about these traps?"** Challenge the students to be alert to these traps and to be honest with themselves. Encourage them to use sensible and positive "self-talk" to help them when they might be about to fall in one of the traps. Point out, *"This is how people develop personal power!"*

14. **Distribute Student Experience Sheet #7, "Avoid these Four Traps!"** The experience sheet offers eight scenarios of students falling into traps and challenges the students to identify which trap is being fallen into in each scenario. Direct the students to work with their partners, or in teams of four, to read the experience sheet together starting with the "Did you know…?" segment at the beginning and then to identify the traps in the scenarios.

Note:

More control may be given to the students to form their own pairings or teams after having been trained on how to proceed and how to honor the ground rules.

Avoid these Four Traps!

Student Experience Sheet #7

Did you know...?

- Certain typical mental and emotional "snares" or "traps" make it difficult for people to make good choices, stay in control of themselves, and manage their anger. Each one usually leads to unpleasant consequences.
- It is easiest to avoid these traps when you know about them.
- **The four traps to avoid are:**
- **Past and present mixups** happen when people think the same painful past event is happening again causing them the same painful upset as before. In truth no two events are exactly the same—only similar.
- **Gunnysacking** is putting up with many upsetting situations over a short time period ("stuffing the gunnysack") without resolving or solving them in some way. Then, when one more irritation occurs the "gunnysacker" angrily erupts.

- **Acting on habit** is the "programmed" way people react to annoyances. They behave the same way every time.
- When a person has **unrealistic expectations** for something that is not realistically obtainable they set themselves up for disappointment and put an unfair strain on others who are expected to deliver what was expected.

Here are four traps to avoid:

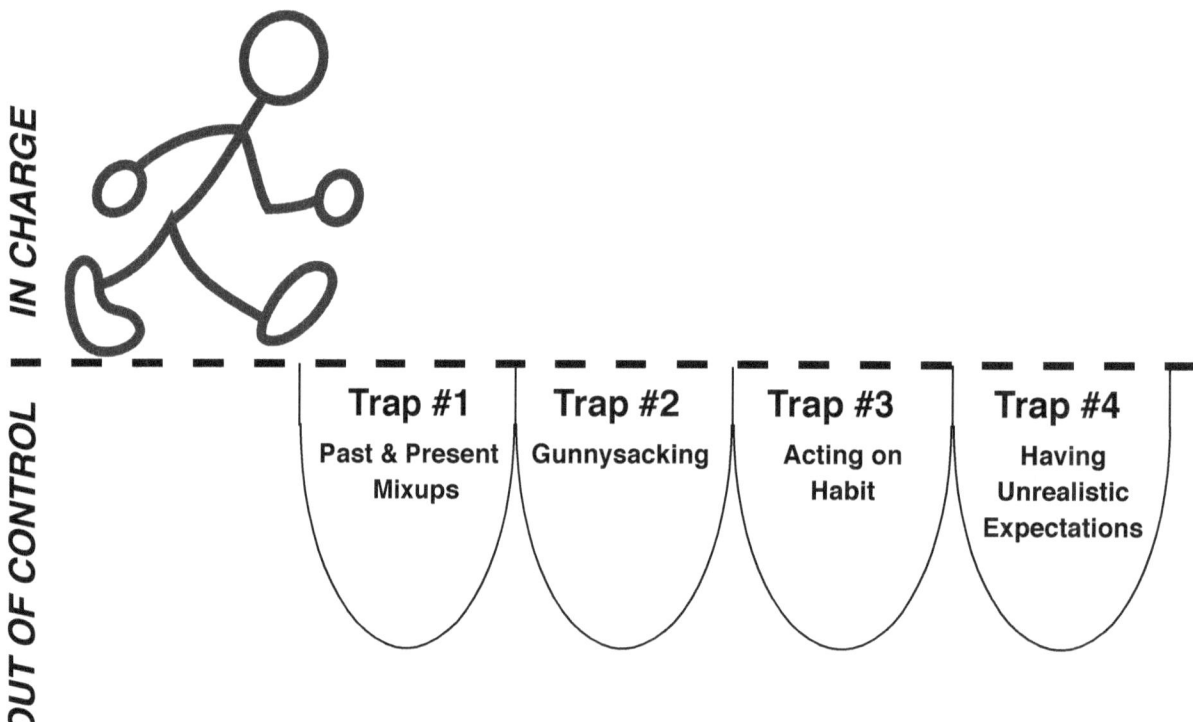

See how well you can identify examples of some students falling in these traps. Read each example, then identify it. Write down the clues you used to reach your conclusion.

1. Liz and her sister, Kate, each blamed the other one morning. Liz blamed Kate for leaving the bathroom in a mess and Kate blamed Liz for taking her jacket without asking first. This sort of thing happens not just in the morning but over and over again all day long almost every day.

   Which trap are Liz and Kate falling into? _____

How can you tell?

_____
_____
_____

2. Darrell bragged that he was sure to get at least a B in English even though he only turned in his homework about half of the time.

   Which trap is Darrell falling into? _____

   How can you tell?

_____
_____
_____

3. Henry's grandfather has had a drinking problem for most of his life but has now been clean and sober for almost a year. Despite this Henry calls his grandfather "the old boozer" whenever he mentions him.

   Which trap is Henry falling into? _____

   How can you tell?

_____
_____
_____

4. Sara's mom always wails the same thing whenever her kids upset her: "Why, oh why, did I have children?"

   Which trap is Sara's mom falling into? _____

How can you tell?

_____

_____

_____

5. John is having a bad day. He didn't get up in time to eat breakfast. He couldn't find a clean shirt to wear. Then he missed the bus. When he sat down in his first class he notices that his pants have yesterday's chocolate syrup on them that he spilled. When his friend says, "You look terrible, man," he loses it and starts yelling.

   Which trap has John fallen into? _____

   How can you tell?

_____

_____

_____

6. Tasha isn't thinking much about her dad who recently lost his job. She's been dropping hints to her parents from the start of December that she wants a new four-piece bedroom set for Christmas.

   Which trap has Tasha fallen into? _____

   How can you tell?

_____

_____

_____

7. Jan came to school with a bad cold. Her nose keeps running and she got a headache. Just thinking straight has become a struggle. Suddenly at lunch she has a coughing spell. Her friend tells her to quit coughing all over the food. Jan bursts into tears and yells at her friend to keep her mouth shut.

   Which trap has Jan fallen into? _____

   How can you tell?

   _____
   _____
   _____

8. Abram is at a family reunion. He won't look at his twenty-year old cousin, Terry, or talk with him because the last time he saw Terry five years ago Terry made fun of him. This time Terry seems to be friendly but Abram is holding a grudge.

   Which trap is Abram falling into? _____

   How can you tell?

   _____
   _____
   _____

Something to remember...

These are very common traps. Almost everyone has probably fallen into each one of them many times. Knowing what they are and how easy it is to fall into them can help you avoid them!

Answers: 1. Liz and Kate: Trap #3; 2. Darrell: Trap #4; 3. Henry: Trap #1; 4. Sara's mom: Trap #3; 5. John: Trap#2; 6. Tasha: Trap #4; 7. Jan: Trap#2; 8. Abram: Trap #1

Lesson 8: Four More Traps to Avoid!

Purpose:

This learning activity closely follows the former one. It helps students understand:

- There are more than four typical mental and emotional "snares" or "traps" that make it difficult at times for people to make good choices, stay in control of themselves, and manage their anger. Just like the first four each one usually leads to unpleasant consequences.
- It is easiest to avoid these traps when you know about them
- **The four traps we will focus on now are:**
- **Unconscious imitation** happens when people who spend time with others imitate the way those people talk and act without realizing it. This isn't healthy when the person being imitated lacks self control and is hurtful to others.
- **Displacement** occurs when angry people take out their anger on others who are innocent and vulnerable because the person(s) who caused the upset hold some kind of power over them.
- **Rationalization** happens when people lie to themselves about why they did or said something unkind in order to dismiss or reduce guilt.
- **Acting out** is out-of-control angry action with no anger management. Examples: throwing a fit, yelling and hitting people or things, and blurting words that hurt—statements that can't be taken back because they were already made.

Materials:

A copy of Student Experience Sheet #8, "Four More Traps to Avoid!" for each student

Preparations:

Draw the picture on the next page on the whiteboard or chart for the students to see as they enter the classroom. (Feel free to add your own "artistic touches" to the figure.)

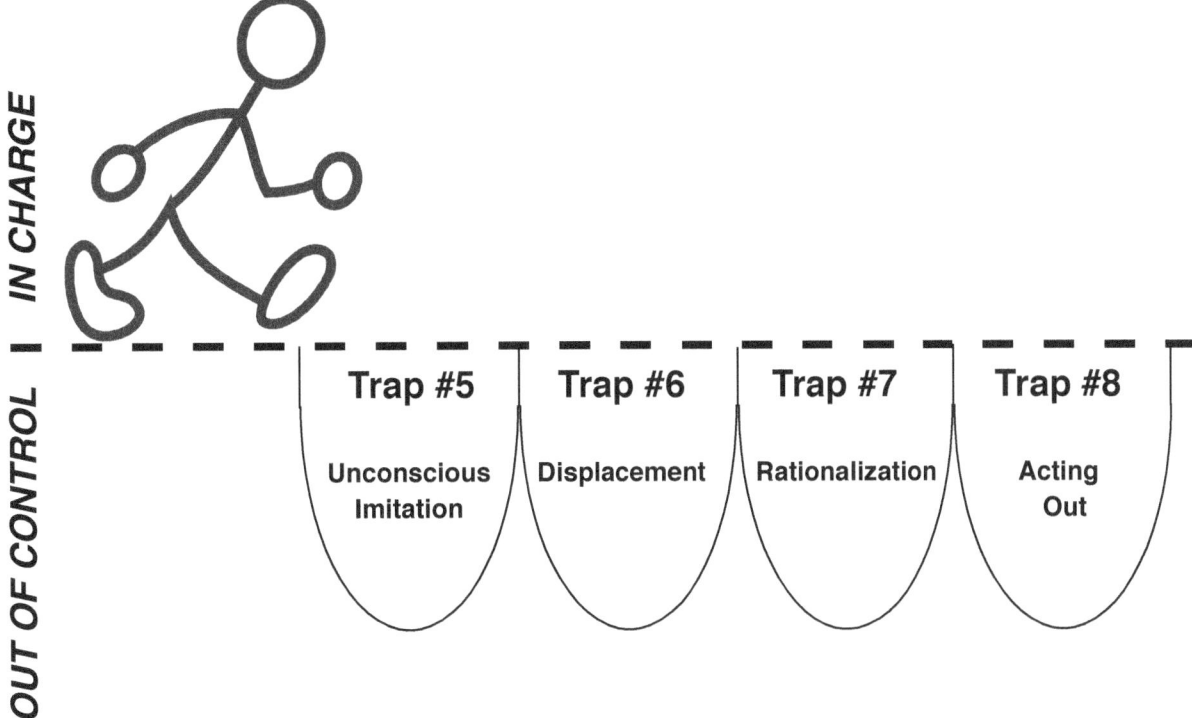

Note:

This learning activity follows Lesson 7, Avoid These Four Traps! which presents traps numbered 1, 2, 3, and 4. For this reason, the additional four traps in this lesson are numbered 5, 6, 7 and 8.

Directions:

1. **Ask the students about the traps they have already learned about:** *"We have been focusing on traps that are easy to fall into when anger is felt. As long as people can stay out of them they are in control. Once they fall into a trap they are below this line (point to line on drawing) and their self-control is gone. That can lead to some very undesirable consequences. What were the traps we focused on in Lesson 7?"* Briefly discuss those four traps: #1 Past & Present Mixups, #2 Gunnysacking, #3 Acting on Habit and #4 Having Unrealistic Expectations.

2. **Announce: *Today we will examine these four additional traps!*** Explain: *"These are ways people act when they have fallen into the traps and have gone out of control. Generally, when they are acting in these ways they don't realize that they are out of control. They know what they are doing but they don't know why. Later they might wonder what happened—how things went wrong. Let's take a look at these four traps."*

3. **Form pairs to discuss the four new traps.** As soon as the students are facing each other, explain: *"I'm going to describe each of these traps. After I describe each one you will have _____ minutes to talk with your partner about it. If you talk about people you know, don't mention their names. Any questions?"*

4. **Point to Trap #5, "Unconscious Imitation."** Describe it: *"Have you ever noticed how much people influence each other? Mainly, people who spend a lot of time with each other tend to act alike—they copy each other's actions and ways of speaking. Younger kids might unconsciously imitate you because they admire you and you might act like some of your friends, older kids, or adults you know. Actually, there's no big problem with unconscious imitation. It's natural. But there IS a problem if you unconsciously imitate people who are frequently out of control and express their anger in ways that hurt other people or themselves. Those are people you want to consciously decide not to imitate. Have you seen or felt examples of this?"*

5. **Direct the students to talk with their partners about "unconscious imitation."** Start them off with, *"Has something like this ever happened to you or have you seen it happen to someone else?"*

6. **Point to Trap #6, "Displacement."** Describe it: *"Have you ever noticed people who are angry with one person take their anger out on someone or something else? That's displacement. In most cases it works like this: someone is angry about something or at someone who has some sort of power over them like a teacher who grades them or a parent who could ground them. So they save their angry energy until they can dump it on a less powerful target like a little sister or the dog. Perhaps this sounds familiar."*

7. **Direct the students to talk with their partners about "displacement."** Start them off with, *"Has something like this ever happened to you or have you seen it happen to someone else?"*

8. **Point to Trap #7, Rationalization.** Describe it: *"This trap is about people fooling themselves. They might even try to fool other people but those people often see through it when rationalizers don't. It's when they tell themselves something that isn't true about why they did something. It could also be a way they tell themselves why they have a certain negative attitude about something or someone. For example, someone steps on another person's foot he's mad at and says, 'Oh sorry. It was an accident.' Then he convinces himself that it was an accident and says to himself, 'But she deserved it.' Does this ring any bells for you?"*

9. **Direct the students to talk with their partners about "rationalization."** Start them off with, *"Has something like this ever happened to you or have you seen it happen to someone else?"*

10. **Point to Trap #8, Acting Out.** Describe it: *"Acting out is just what it sounds like. It's very obvious, out-of-control behavior such as throwing a fit, yelling and hitting things or people, and blurting remarks that hurt--statements that can't be taken back because they were already made. (The only thing acting out might be better than is swallowing anger and pretending that everything's fine which is like swallowing poison that stays in the system.) The worst thing about acting out is that when people do it they make themselves look bad and don't earn anyone's respect even though they may feel powerful at the time. That feeling is an illusion. Most of the time people look disgusting or ridiculous when they're acting out. Can you relate to this?"*

11. **Direct the students to talk with their partners about "acting out."** Start them off with, *"Has something like this ever happened to you or have you seen it happen to someone else?"*

12. **Point out, *We've talked about eight anger traps but there are more. Can you think of any others?*** Listen to their responses perhaps adding their traps to the drawing and labelling them.

13. **Finally ask, "How is it helpful to know about these traps?"** As before in Lesson #7, challenge the students to be alert to these traps and to be honest with themselves. Remind them that avoiding these traps is an important way to develop self-control and personal power.

14. **Distribute Student Experience Sheet #8, "Four More Traps to Avoid!"** The experience sheet offers eight new scenarios featuring the same students falling into the four additional traps. It challenges them to identify which trap is being fallen into in each one. Direct the students to work with their partners, or in teams of four, to read the experience sheet together starting with the "Did you know...?" segment at the beginning, and then to identify the traps in the scenarios.

Four More Traps to Avoid!

Student Experience Sheet #8

Did you know...?

- There are more than four typical mental and emotional "snares" or "traps" that make it difficult at times for people to make good choices, stay in control of themselves, and manage their anger. Just like the first four each one usually leads to unpleasant consequences.
- It is easiest to avoid these traps when you know about them
- **The four traps we will focus on now are:**
- **Unconscious imitation** happens when people who spend time with others imitate the way those people talk and act without realizing it. This isn't healthy when the person being imitated lacks self control and is hurtful to others.
- **Displacement** occurs when angry people take out their anger on others who are innocent and vulnerable because the person(s) who caused the upset hold some kind of power over them.
- **Rationalization** happens when people lie to themselves about why they did or said something unkind in order to dismiss or reduce guilt.
- **Acting out** is out-of-control angry action with no anger management. Examples: throwing a fit, yelling and hitting people or things, and blurting words that hurt—statements that can't be taken back because they were already made.

Four more traps to avoid:

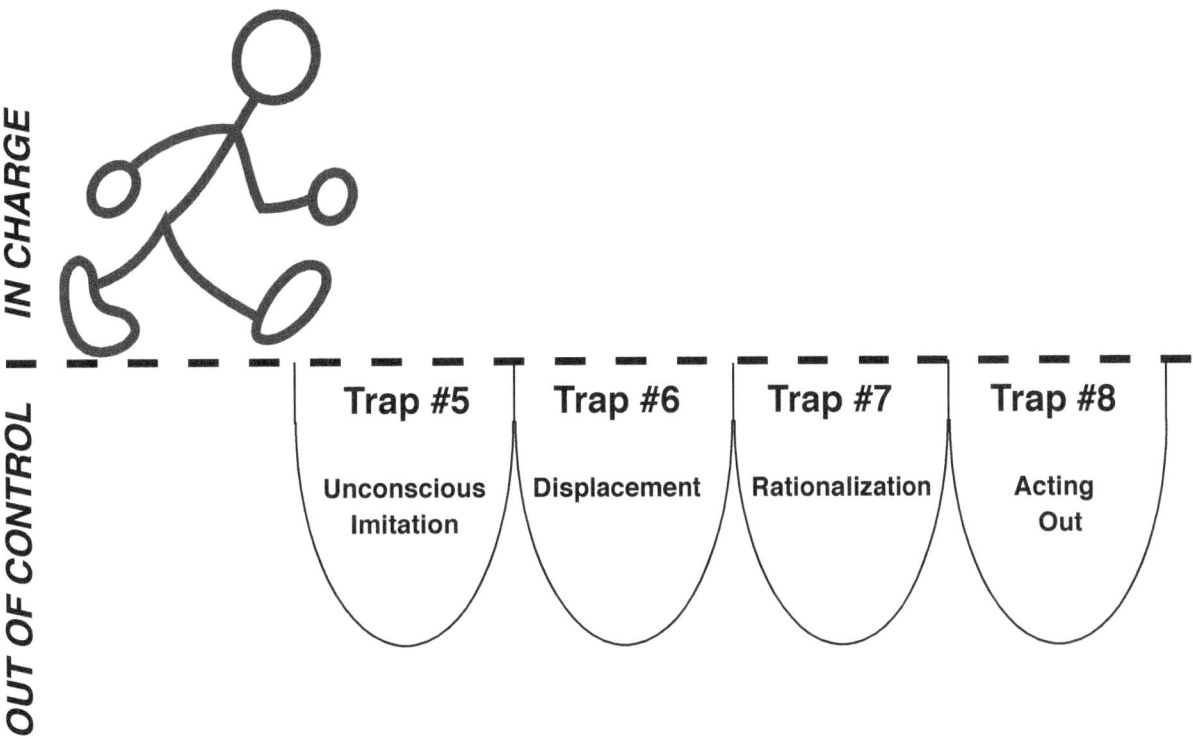

See how well you can identify examples of the same students falling in these traps. Read each example then identify it. Write down the clues you used to reach your conclusion.

1. Liz got into the bus too slowly to suit the bus driver this afternoon who told her to step on it. This annoyed her. When she got home she yelled at her younger sister, Kate, for drinking the last of the milk.

    Which trap did Liz fall into? _____

    How can you tell?

    _____
    _____
    _____

2. Darrell got a D in English because he only turned in his homework about half of the time. Now he's telling his friends he doesn't care.

   Which trap is Darrell falling into? _____

   How can you tell?

   _____
   _____
   _____

3. Henry doesn't like what his mom wants him to wear to his cousin's birthday party. He becomes verbally abusive, calling his mom some very bad names and telling her to get out of his life.

   Which trap is Henry falling into? _____

   How can you tell?

   _____
   _____
   _____

4. Sara's mom always says the same thing with agony whenever her kids upset her: "Why, oh why, did I have children?" Now Sara is babysitting her neighbor's four-year old who jumped in some mud. Sara wails, "Why, oh why did I take this job?"

   Which trap is Sara falling into? _____

   How can you tell?

   _____
   _____
   _____

5. John sees another bad day coming. Once again he isn't getting up on time to have any breakfast and he's likely to miss the bus. His alarm didn't go off. John throws the alarm clock across the room. It hits the wall and shatters.

   Which trap has John fallen into? _____

   How can you tell?

   _____
   _____
   _____

6. Tasha didn't get the new four-piece bedroom set she wanted for Christmas. She goes into a sulk not speaking to anyone just like her older sister does whenever she doesn't get what she wants.

   Which trap has Tasha fallen into? _____

   How can you tell?

   _____
   _____
   _____

7. Jan has a bad cold. At lunch she coughed all over her food and her friend's food. When her friend objects Jan bursts into tears and yells at her friend to keep her mouth shut. Then she goes into a fury calling her friend a royal pain and stomps out of the lunch room.

   Which trap has Jan fallen into? _____

   How can you tell?

   _____
   _____
   _____

8. Abram freezes when he sees his older cousin, Terry, coming towards him at the family reunion because he still has a bad feeling about Terry. His cousin smiles and says, "How are you doing, Abram? Hey, is anything wrong?" Abram won't admit to himself or anyone else that he's still feeling hurt about the way Terry treated him five years ago. He responds, "No, no! I couldn't wait to see you."

Which trap is Abram falling into? _____

How can you tell?

_____
_____
_____

Something to remember...

These are four more very common traps. Like the first four you looked at, almost everyone has probably fallen into each one of them many times. It can be useful to know about all eight of the traps and how easy it is to fall into them. This helps you avoid them!

Answers: 1. Liz: Trap #6; 2. Darrell: Trap #7; 3. Henry: Trap #8; 4. Sara: Trap #5; 5. John: Trap #6; 6. Tasha: Trap #5; 7. Jan: Trap #8; 8. Abram: Trap #7

Lesson 9: Grudges are Poison

Purpose:

This learning activity helps students understand:
- When you have a grievance it might be based on unfair treatment you received or it may be something you are imagining or blowing out of proportion in your mind.
- A grievance turns into a grudge if you are giving lots of your mental time and energy to it. You are also "swallowing" poison if you keep thinking negative thoughts about it without trying to resolve or solve it in some way.
- When you hold a grudge against someone you are giving them control over you by allowing them to occupy your mind.
- You can decide that holding a grudge isn't worth the damage it causes you.
- It can be hard but forgiving others can free your mind and lift your spirit. (You can do it inside your head.)

Materials:

A copy of the Student Experience Sheet #9, "Grudges are Poison" for each student

Preparations:

Write these words on the whiteboard: **GRIEVANCE, GRUDGE, OBSESSION, FORGIVENESS**

Directions:

1. **Initiate the activity by asking the students," Did you know that it's possible to swallow your own poison?"** Explain: *"That's what we're going to focus on today. I'm about to read a short story from your experience sheet to you. The title is, 'The Wolves Inside Us.' You may choose to close your eyes and listen."*

2. **Point out: "The last line of the story will be missing.** Explain: *"I'll tell you what it is after you have discussed your thoughts about it with your partners."*

3. **Read the story, "The Wolves Inside Us" aloud from the student experience sheet and printed in this book.** Encourage the students to listen and focus carefully.

4. **Challenge the students to think about what the last line of the story might be.** Explain: *"Without speaking, take a few moments to think about what you imagine the grandfather said in answer to his grandson's question."*

   (You may receive requests to repeat the last part of the story which could help the students clarify in their minds what the grandfather might have said. If this occurs, start with, "The boy looked intently ...")

5. **Give the students a clue:** After a few moments, you could add: *"I'll give you a tip: his statement is four words long and it has to do with food!"*

6. **Call on four or five students to state what they think the four words might have been.** Listen to their ideas with a nod. (It's unlikely that they will know the four words unless they have heard this story already.)

7. **Tell the students the last line of the story:** "The grandfather smiled and quietly said: **"The One I Feed."**

8. **Form pairs and distribute copies of the Student Experience Sheet #9, "Grudges are Poison."** Suggest they write the last four words of the story in the blanks on their experience sheets.

9. **Direct the pairs to talk about what the last line means:** *"Talk with your partner about what you think the grandfather meant with these four words. You have _____ minutes."*

10. **Call on several students to explain what they think "The one I feed," means.** Listen to, and acknowledge, each explanation.

11. **Challenge the students to grasp the full meaning:** *"Let's get totally clear on the meaning of 'The one I feed.' Take notes on your experience sheet. It has the questions I'm about to ask."*

    —*"Since the two wolves are imaginary how can they be 'fed'?"* (We feed these imaginary wolves with our thoughts.)

    —*"By thinking a lot about the bad parts of something someone said or did that upset you, how are you 'feeding' hateful and angry feelings?"* (We feed ourselves poison when we do this. It's proven to be a chemical process that damages the physical body.)

    —*"How might you feed the wolf who prefers to live in harmony with others?"* (We could wait until everyone has settled down then tell the people who hurt us how it made us feel and express a desire to continue being friends without the hurtful actions. When we feel better we could also forgive them in our minds.)

12. **Focus on the vocabulary.** Ask the following questions and listen to the students' responses. Clarify as necessary using the statements shown under each question.

   — *"What is a GRIEVANCE?"* "
   "Is it always wrong to have a grievance?" No. Some grievances are phoney—products of someone's imagination. But others are legitimate like being blamed for something you didn't do. Either way, when it is on the mind a lot and nothing is being done to solve the problem, it is likely to turn into a grudge.

   — *"What is a GRUDGE?"*
   "Why are grudges unhealthy?" A grudge is a collection of hurt, scared, angry, hateful feelings and memories of what caused those feelings that people keep going over again and again in their minds. It is unhealthy because they are continually "swallowing poison." Grudges are also prone to cause vengeful actions which make things worse.

   — *"What is an OBSESSION?"*
   An obsession is thinking constantly about something that arouses constant feelings of a certain type. When people hold grudges they obsess on hurtful memories and negative thoughts that produce painful feelings.

   — *"What is FORGIVENESS?"*
   Forgiveness is the process of giving up resentment and anger against a person or group. It can be done with spoken words or just inside the mind. Forgiving someone doesn't mean that you will let them hurt you again.

13. **Suggest:** *Take a few more minutes to read and discuss the five point "Let's review ..." segment on your experience sheets with your partner.*

14. **Close the activity by sharing your vision with the students:** *"I have a vision of each of you in my mind's eye feeding your own good wolf with positive thoughts and sending the bad one into the woods with his tail between his legs!"*

Grudges are Poison

Student Experience Sheet #9

THE WOLVES INSIDE US

An angry Native American boy sat quietly fuming by the side of a creek when his grandfather walked by. He called out to his grandfather asking him to come and talk with him. Right away the grandfather could tell that his grandson was upset about something. He asked him what was wrong.

The boy was glad that someone cared how he felt. He responded by telling his grandfather what one of his so-called friends had done to him that was mean and disrespectful. He explained that he just couldn't stop thinking about it and the more he thought about it the more hateful and angry he felt. As the boy told his story, his grandfather listened to every word.

Then the boy's grandfather spoke, "I see that you have a reasonable grievance but now it's turning into a grudge and making you miserable. I, too, have felt great anger and hate toward people who have taken so much and not been ashamed of their actions.

But concentrating on feelings like that without telling your friend how you feel about what he did only hurts you, not the one who did you the injustice. It's like taking poison and wishing your enemy would die."

The boy's grandfather continued: "I have struggled with these kinds of feelings many times. It's as if there are two wolves living inside me. One is good and never harms anyone. He lives in harmony with his surroundings and does not become offended when no offense was intended. In his mind he forgives other people for not being perfect because he knows he's not perfect either. He only fights when he has to and he does it fairly.

"But the other wolf...ah!" the grandfather went on, "the littlest thing sends him into a rage. He is disagreeable and resentful. He fights others for no reason. He can't think straight because the grudges he's holding cloud his mind. His anger-driven behavior is useless because it only makes things worse. It's difficult to live sometimes with these two wolves inside me. Each one wants to control my spirit."

The boy looked intently into his grandfather's eyes and asked, "Grandfather, which one wins?"

The grandfather smiled and softly said, "____ ____ __ ____."

What do you think the boy's grandfather meant with these four words?

_____
_____
_____
_____
_____

How could imaginary wolves be "fed?"

_____
_____
_____
_____
_____

By thinking a lot about the bad parts of something someone said or did that upset you, how are you "feeding" hateful and angry feelings?

_____
_____
_____
_____
_____

How might you feed the wolf who prefers to live in harmony with others?

_____
_____
_____
_____
_____

Let's review ...

- When you have a grievance it might be based on unfair treatment you received or it may be something you are imagining or blowing out of proportion in your mind.
- A grievance turns into a grudge if you are giving lots of your mental time and energy to it. You are also "swallowing" poison if you keep thinking negative thoughts about it without trying to resolve or solve it in some way.
- When you hold a grudge against someone you are giving them control over you by allowing them to occupy your mind.
- You can decide that holding a grudge isn't worth the damage it causes you.
- It can be hard but forgiving others can free your mind and lift your spirit. (You can do it inside your head.)

Lesson 10: Revenge Is Not Sweet for Long!

Purpose:

This learning activity helps students understand ,,,

- The urge to get even with someone who has wronged you or someone you care about is very common and can be very strong.
- Revenge often results from holding a grudge.
- When wronged, the urge to "get even" may be strong, but the act of taking revenge frequently backfires.
- When someone wrongs you there are better ways of dealing with it than getting even or obsessing about getting even.

Materials:

A copy of the Student Experience Sheet #9, "Revenge Is Not Sweet for Long!" for each student

Computers, laptops or I-Pads with internet access and/or library resources

Preparations:

For Part One, write these words on the whiteboard:

INSULT	RESENTMENT	ANIMOSITY	REVENGE
FEUD	WAR	REPERCUSSIONS	BOOMERANG
ESCALATION	BACKFIRES	OUT-OF-CONTROL	
	COUNTER PRODUCTIVE.		

Directions:

Part One:

1. **Intrigue the students with a personal story about "getting even."**
Describe an instance in your own life that you would feel comfortable sharing which involved a time you were wronged and felt a desire to "get even" with the individual who wronged you, but after taking the action, found that your revenge was not sweet for long. This might be one from the time in your life when you were the age of your students. If you do not

feel comfortable sharing such a story, tell them about something of this kind that happened to someone else without naming the individual. Use as many of the words written on the whiteboard as you can and point to them as you tell your story.

2. **Point out the terms on the whiteboard and discuss their meaning.**
   Then explain: *"The urge to get even when someone has hurt you, or someone you care about, is very common and can be strongly felt. But if revenge is actually taken by 'getting back' at the person who acted first, there are frequently bad boomerangs and backfires and they can happen fast."*

3. **Describe how revenge can be the result of "mental mixups:"**
   "Sometimes people can become extremely unreasonable with the urge to get even. The situation might not even involve them. For example: someone insults your brother and after you hear about it, you feel angry every time you see anyone in that person's family. Can you relate to this sort of mental mixup?"

4. **Ask the students** if they know of any stories about nonfictional historical figures or fictional characters who became swept up in the urge to avenge themselves or someone they cared about for having been wronged which may have led to serious feuds and repercussions. Brainstorm a list. It could include:

   Nonfictional Feuds:
   - Alexander Hamilton and Aaron Burr
   - Billy the Kid and Pat Garrett
   - The Hatfields and the McCoys
   - Wyatt Earp and the Clantons

   Fictional Feuds:
   - The Capulets and the Montagues from William Shakespeare's *Romeo and Juliet*
   - Captain Ahab and the White Whale from Herman Melville's *Moby Dick*
   - Dr. Frankenstein and the Monster from Mary Shelley's, *Frankenstein*
   - The Grangerfords and the Shepherdsons from *The Adventures of Huckleberry Finn* by Mark Twain

5. **Assign research teams with each team selecting its own topic.** Distribute Student Experience Sheet #10. "Revenge Is Not Sweet for Long!" Ask a student to read the "Did you know...?" statements at the top and another student to read the next two paragraphs. Then explain: *"Your team will have _____ class period(s) to research the stories of the people you are investigating--how one party wronged the other, the revenge that took place back and forth, and what the final outcome was. Use your experience sheet to help you write down the key information and to come to the most reasonable conclusions. Your team reports will be made on (name the day). Any questions?"*

Part Two:

6. **Students conduct their research.** As they investigate their topics using the internet and the library, coach and consult with them as needed. Suggest that they might find ways to be creative by adding short readings from literature, songs, and art to illustrate and augment their presentations.

7. **Help with presentation planning.** Remind the students to find a way for each member of their team to participate in presenting their report to the class. Suggest they give each member at least one segment from the guidelines in the experience sheet.

Part Three:

8. **Facilitate the reports:** Call on each team to report on its topic to the class following the sequence of the investigation guidelines on their experience sheet as it is useful to them. Direct them to introduce their presentation with an explanation of the characters who participated in the feud, the time frame and the setting before going into what happened.

9. **Close the activity by asking the students:** *"It's been said that revenge is sweet. Do you agree?"* Guide the discussion on how revenge is generally not sweet for long, but leads instead to escalation, backfires and repercussions. Frequently the ultimate result is misery for everyone involved as well as those "caught in the crossfire."

Revenge Is Not Sweet for Long!

Student Experience Sheet #10

Did you know...?
- The urge to get even with someone who has wronged you or someone you care about is very common and can be very strong.
- Revenge often results from holding a grudge.
- When wronged, the urge to "get even" may seem overpowering, but the act of taking revenge frequently backfires.
- When someone wrongs you there are better ways of dealing with it than getting even or obsessing about getting even.

Since the beginning of recorded history there have been stories—fictional and nonfictional—about humans at war with other humans based on hatred and the urge to get even. It's a part of human nature that has caused so much misery it can't be measured. It still goes on today. No one who gets involved really wins because the violence itself—even verbal violence—is destructive to the human spirit for everyone involved.

Besides wars, history is full of feuds which are fights between individuals or small groups like families who have fought to get even with their enemies. Here are four famous stories of actual feuds from history:

Nonfictional Feuds:
- Alexander Hamilton and Aaron Burr
- Billy the Kid and Pat Garrett
- The Hatfields and the McCoys
- Wyatt Earp and the Clantons

Literature is also full of wars and feuds—fights between people who hate each other and keep trying to get revenge. Here are four famous fictional stories:

Fictional Feuds:

- The Capulets and the Montagues from William Shakespeare's *Romeo and Juliet*
- Captain Ahab and the White Whale from Herman Melville's *Moby Dick*
- Dr. Frankenstein and the Monster from Mary Shelley's *Frankenstein*
- The Grangerfords and the Shepherdsons from Mark Twain's *The Adventures of Huckleberry Finn*

Join a research team and pick a nonfictional or fictional story to investigate. Use the investigation guidelines below to help you write the important information you discover about the feud your team is investigating. Here's some vocabulary that can help:

Insult	**revenge**	**animosity**
resentment	**war**	**feud**
repercussions	**escalation**	**backfires**
boomerang	**out-of-control**	**counter productive**

Write in other useful vocabulary here:

_____   _____

_____   _____

_____   _____

_____   _____

_____   _____

Investigation Guidelines:

Read your source material and write your responses to these questions which can help you organize your team's report in a logical sequence.

1. Who fought whom?

   _____

2. When did it happen? ...and where?

   _____
   _____

3. How did the feud start?

   _____
   _____
   _____
   _____

4. Who caused animosity and resentment in the other and in what ways?

   _____
   _____
   _____
   _____

5. Who wanted to get revenge first? Did it work?

   _____
   _____

6. Who went out-of-control and in what way?

_____

_____

7. How did the feud keep escalating?

_____

_____

_____

8. How did the actions of the fighters boomerang on them?

_____

_____

9. In what ways did both sides lose? Did anyone else suffer too?

_____

_____

Question: What did you learn from this investigation and listening to the other teams' reports that was important for you?

_____

_____

_____

_____

_____

_____

Lesson 11: Start Out Fresh!

Purpose:

This learning activity helps students understand:

- Depression is often caused by anger turned inward.
- Sometimes anger turned inward is a poisonous grudge we hold against ourselves for mistakes we have made.
- Mistakes are best seen as errors that we can decide not to repeat; often these errors can be corrected with helpful actions.
- Apologizing and/or expressing regret is one way to correct errors that have hurt or offended others.
- Mistakes made in the past can be useful as teachers, but punishing ourselves with guilt is not useful.

Materials:

A copy of the Student Experience Sheet #11, "Start Out Fresh!" for each student

Directions:

1. **Begin by asking the students, "*Have you ever held a grudge against yourself?*** *Don't answer out loud. Sometimes in all of our lives we make mistakes that we feel guilty about especially if we hurt someone in some way. I have a story I'd like us to read together about a situation like this that happened many years ago."*

2. **Distribute copies of the Student Experience Sheet #11 "Start Out Fresh!"** Then read the story aloud from the experience sheet in the book as the students close their eyes and listen or silently read along.

3. **Ask the students, "*What are the messages of this story?*"** Listen to their responses, then add: *"For some people, grudges held against themselves are even more poisonous than grudges they hold against others. Many people are much harder on themselves than on anyone else for mistakes they have made. Perhaps this is true for you. But as the grandmother in the story pointed out, you only damage yourself when you punish yourself with blame and guilt for errors. Let mistakes be your teachers. If you have hurt someone have the courage to tell them you are sorry. The benefit for you is a fresh start. Having the courage to apologize or at least express regret is another way to build personal power."*

4. **Explain:** "*Your experience sheets are just for you this time.* They give you some questions about an error you may have made and how you might correct it. What you write is personal. It's not to be shared with anyone unless you choose to. Take some time to read and write in it now."

5. **Before closing the lesson read the "Let's Review ..." segment at the end of the experience sheets together.** Ask for the students' comments and acknowledge their contributions.

Start Out Fresh!

Student Experience Sheet #11

LET MISTAKES BE YOUR TEACHERS

A Native American grandmother noticed that her granddaughter, Brown Pebble, seemed withdrawn and depressed. She went to her and asked, "What's wrong, my child?"

"Nothing," answered the granddaughter.

"Come now, my dear," the grandmother said. "It is clear that something is troubling you. Why don't you trust me and tell me what it is?"

Sadly and with embarrassment, Brown Pebble spoke: "I can't seem to do anything right. The other girls are much better cooks than I am. They can tan hides and weave better than me. I can't even build a decent fire. And when they tease me I become angry and full of hatred. Yesterday I screamed at Dancing Fox and slapped her. Then I ran off. Now I feel terrible about it. What's wrong with me?"

The girl's grandmother was quiet for a moment, then said, "I remember times like that when I was a girl. I felt everyone was better than I was and that I was the only one who doubted myself. I got angry very easily and did things to hurt people I resented and then I regretted it later."

Brown Pebble looked at her and asked, "But grandmother, now you are so content and everyone loves you. What happened?"

With tears in her eyes, the old grandmother smiled and said, "I went to my grandmother. I'll tell you what she told me. 'Let mistakes be your teachers for they are the best teachers.' In time, you will learn to do your tasks well enough. It doesn't matter if others have learned faster than you. And don't hold grudges against yourself when you have wronged someone. Instead of obsessing on your guilty feelings do something to correct the error. Go to Dancing Fox, admit your poor behavior, and tell her you are sorry for it. This takes courage but it also frees your spirit of self-blame and guilt. Don't damage yourself anymore. Get a fresh start!"

To thank her grandmother for this gift of words Brown Pebble quietly bowed. The next time she saw Dancing Fox she said, "I'm sorry I screamed and slapped you." Dancing Fox stared at her for a few moments. Then she said, "We were teasing you. I guess we shouldn't have done that. I'm sorry too."

As Brown Pebble walked away she noticed how much better she felt inside.

Does this story about Brown Pebble remind you of anything you've personally done or felt? Here's a chance to "talk with yourself" (in writing) about it. Keeping what you write only for yourself because it's private, fill in your responses to these questions:

An error I wish I hadn't made that hurt someone was:

_____

_____

_____

_____

_____

How I was feeling at the time:

_____

_____

_____

How I feel about it now:

_____
_____
_____

How I corrected the error, or if I haven't corrected it what could I do now to correct it?

_____
_____
_____
_____

In what ways can I coach myself to correct mistakes I make with other people? What are some helpful things I could say to myself? What are some things I could do or stop doing?

_____
_____
_____
_____

Let's Review ...

- Depression is often caused by anger turned inward.
- Sometimes anger turned inward is a poisonous grudge we hold against ourselves for mistakes we have made.
- Mistakes are best seen as errors that we can decide not to repeat; often these errors can be corrected with helpful actions.
- Apologizing and/or expressing regret is one way to correct errors that have hurt or offended others.
- Mistakes made in the past can be useful as teachers, but punishing ourselves with guilt is not useful.

Lesson 12: Use Your Anger—Don't Let It Use You!

Purpose:

This learning activity helps students understand:

- Angry energy can be channelled to bring about constructive actions where no one gets hurt.

- First acknowledge the anger. Then stop yourself from doing something harmful like acting out or letting yourself become depressed. Next, be your own coach. Decide and plan to use the energy your anger gives you to your advantage.

- Using anger, instead of letting it use you, is one of the highest expressions of self-control and anger management! It's a great way to build personal power!

Materials:

A copy of the Student Experience Sheet #12, "Use Your Anger—Don't Let it Use You!" for each student

Directions:

Part One:

1. **Initiate the activity by telling the class a personal story.** Your story could be about a time you were angry and used the energy your anger gave you to do something important that you might otherwise have given up on doing. It could be a recent experience like going to court to plead innocence to a speeding ticket when you weren't actually speeding-- the judge believed you and cancelled the fine. Or it might have been something you accomplished with the help of angry energy when you were the age of your students.

2. **Dramatize your story with the help of some of the students.** Surprise the students by asking one or more to take roles in a brief drama depicting your story. Narrate the drama and tell the class, as an aside, how you are feeling at each point in the drama. Have fun with the students as you do this.

3. **Emphasize that you actually used the energy your anger gave you.** Point out that you did what was needed while hurting no one in the process.

4. **Distribute Student Experience Sheet #12, "Use Your Anger—Don't Let It Use You!"** Explain that you would like the students to close their eyes and listen or read along silently as you read the story aloud from the student experience sheet entitled, "She Used Her Anger Well."

5. **Form pairs to respond to two important questions on the experience sheets.** As soon as the students are facing each other ask the first question. Give them enough time to discuss it. Repeat the process with the second question.

    - *"What do you think of Jane's actions?"*

    - *"How did her anger actually help her? What could she have said to herself that would have defeated her?"*

6. **Challenge the students:** *You can use your anger too instead of letting it use you!* Add: *"In fact, you may not have realized it, or given yourself credit for it, but you probably have done this yourself."* Point out the next question on the experience sheet which leads into tomorrow's activity."

7. **Explain tomorrow's activity:** *"Tomorrow we will form teams of four. The topic will be, 'A Time I Used My Anger Instead of Letting It Use Me' so search your memory of times you did this. Also, during the time between now and class tomorrow you may get angry about something and decide to use the energy your anger gives you to achieve something constructive while hurting no one. That's also something you could tell your team about. Each team will pick one story to dramatize for the class."*

Part Two (the next day):

8. **Direct the students to re-form their teams to discuss the topic, "A Time I Used My Anger Instead of Letting It Use Me."** Provide sufficient time for them to share their stories with their teammates.

9. **Give directions to the students for planning their dramatizations.** Ask the teams to select one of the stories they heard to dramatize in front of the class. Explain that the student who shared the story should play him or herself and also direct the action, assigning parts to other members of his or her team. Give the teams time for planning their dramatizations.

10. **Set the stage for the dramatizations.** Before beginning each dramatization, ask the student with the story to describe the setting and situation. Encourage the student to tell the audience what he or she is feeling and saying to him or herself during the action. To the extent needed, help with narration while each scenario is dramatized. At the end of each one, ask the student who shared the story, *"How did using the energy your anger gave you so well cause you to feel about yourself?"*

11. **Conclude the lesson** by directing the student's attention to the "Let's review..." segment at the end of their experience sheet. Ask them to read and discuss it with their teammates.

Use Your Anger—Don't Let It Use You!

Student Experience Sheet #12

SHE USED HER ANGER WELL!

Jane is a 10th grader. She's learning to play the clarinet and is starting to get good at it. Her school has a music club that jams after school two days a week. She seriously wants to join it. Most of the members are in the 12th grade. In order to be selected as a 10th grader, Jane has to have much better grades and be recommended, in writing, by at least two teachers.

When Jane found this out she was discouraged and angry. She thought it just wasn't right or fair to keep younger kids with average grades like her out. The next day she talked with one of her musical friends, Suli, who was having the same feelings about it. "Let's just forget it. The rules are stupid," Suli said. "You and I don't have a chance."

But later that week, Jane made a decision to try her best. It took time. She paid better attention in class, always did her homework, got help from her mom and older brother when she got stuck on hard assignments and as a result her grades went up. But then Jane had to get those recommendations. Just the thought of going to two teachers and asking for letters of recommendation made her feel like giving up. Was it shyness? Fear? Or maybe it was the idea that she was being "too good?" Whatever it was, she held back for days.

But then Jane made the move. What got her to do it? The anger! She reminded herself of how mad she felt about having to do all these things and that gave her the energy and courage she needed. The next day she asked her teacher, Mr. Smith, if she could talk with him in private. He said, "Sure. Let's talk today right after class," so they did and he said he'd be happy to write her a letter of recommendation.

Then Jane realized: "I can talk with Mrs. Greenway," another one of her teachers, "she's friends with Mr. Smith. I'll tell her he's writing one." The plan worked and worked well! It took two more weeks but at the next meeting of the music club Jane was selected to become a new member.

What do you think of Jane's actions?"

_____
_____
_____
_____
_____
_____

How did her anger actually help her? What could she have said to herself that would have defeated her?

_____
_____
_____
_____
_____
_____

Can you remember a time when you used your anger instead of letting it use you? Write down how you did it here:

_____
_____
_____
_____
_____
_____
_____
_____
_____
_____

Let's review ...

- Angry energy can be channelled to bring about constructive actions where no one gets hurt.
- First acknowledge the anger. Then stop yourself from doing something harmful like acting out or letting yourself become depressed. Next, be your own coach. Decide and plan to use the energy your anger gives you to your advantage.
- Using anger, instead of letting it use you, is one of the highest expressions of self-control and anger management! It's a great way to build personal power!

Lesson 13: You've Got the Power!

Purpose:

This learning activity helps students understand:

- Conscious deep breathing strengthens the power of self-control in difficult situations.
- Using your mind to visualize positive outcomes in difficult situations helps you manage your anger and make those outcomes happen.
- Awareness that you possess the personal power to control yourself and manage your anger enables you to use it.

Materials:

A copy of the Student Experience Sheet #13, "You've Got the Power!" for each student

Preparations:

Tie the lightest end of a common one-inch metal paper clip to a sewing thread for each student. The length of the thread from the fingers holding it to the paper clip should be 15 inches. (This is important.) The short end of thread extending from the knot on the paper clip should be snipped off.

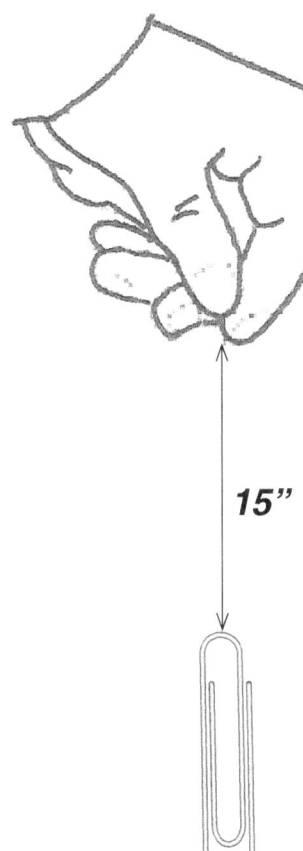

15"

Notes:

Prepare the students (perhaps the day before) by telling them that you are going to ask them to think of a recent situation that annoyed them for the next lesson. Add that they will not be asked to talk about it—just to keep it in mind.

It is recommended that you try the experiments in this lesson by yourself before doing them with the class in order to know first-hand what to anticipate.

Directions:

1. **Begin by announcing, "*Today we're going to demonstrate our personal power!*"** Add: *"Believe it or not, all we're going to need is a paper clip and a piece of thread for two amazing experiments! Each experiment has two parts."*

2. **Distribute the paper clips attached to the threads.** (You may choose to allow the students to tie their own paper clips to the threads using the guidelines stated under Preparations.)

3. **Conduct the first step of the first experiment.** Ask the students to grasp their thread with their dominant hand at the end of the 15 inches in order to dangle the paper clip so it hangs down as far as possible without touching anything. Also they should not brace their arms on their desks or any firm surface.

    Explain: *"Try your best to keep the paper clip from swaying while you listen to my voice."* As soon as everyone is ready, continue: *"Close your eyes and think back to a recent time when you became angry. Remember what happened that upset you and exactly how you felt. Keep thinking about it for a few more moments.* (Pause for about 10 more seconds.) *"Now open your eyes. What is your paper clip doing?"*

    Ask the students to describe what they see. In most cases the students' paper clips will be noticeably swaying.

4. **Conduct the second step of the first experiment; add deep breathing.** Repeat the procedure used for the first step in exactly the same way with one difference. Direct the students: *"As we begin this second step, take a slow deep breath in through your nose and out through your mouth as you close your eyes. Don't brace your arm on anything. Continue to breathe in and out deeply and slowly for a few more moments as you try to keep your paper clip from swaying and as you think again about the situation that angered you—the same one you thought about before."* At the end of about 10 more seconds, direct the students to take one more deep breath in and out, then open their eyes. Your question to them is the same: *"What is your paper clip doing?"*

    Ask the students to report what they see and how it differs from what they saw before. In most cases the students' paper clips will be swaying much less noticeably or not at all.

5. **Derive meaning by asking the students:**
    — *"Did breathing deeply the second time make a difference?"*
    — *"Did you expect this to happen?"*
    — *"What does this tell you about how you could use your own breathing to help stay in control and steady yourself when you become angry?"*

6. **Ask:** *"Did you know that most people stop breathing normally when they are stressed?"* Elaborate: *"I asked you to think about something that angered you. When people just think about something that upset them it stresses them causing their breathing to become shallow. Some people in extremely upsetting situations almost strangle themselves without realizing it. In some cases they have panic attacks or even pass out! When people don't breathe normally their ability to think clearly and make good judgements are reduced because their brains aren't getting enough oxygen.*

   "The good news is that you can remember to breathe deeply like you did in the second step of the experiment in tense situations that anger you. Your own breath gives you a lot of help. If you combine that with positive self-talk you have a good chance of controlling yourself and choosing to do something that you would feel okay about later."

7. **Distribute copies of Student Experience Sheet #13, "You've Got the Power!"** Give the students a few minutes to fill in their written responses to questions 1 through 5.

8. **Conduct the first step of the second experiment.** Direct the students to dangle their paper clips exactly as they did before but this time they should brace their elbows on a surface. Tell them, *"You can think about anything while we do this. Take hold of the paper clip with your other hand to make it stay still. As soon as it's still remove that hand from it. Keep your eyes open this time. Do your best to keep your paper clip from moving by keeping your arm and hand steady. Also use your mind to keep it steady by intending that it should not move and by seeing it staying perfectly still."* (Repeat these last two sentences slowly.)

   Pause for about 10 more seconds then ask, *"What is your paper clip doing?"* In most cases the students' paper clips will be still.

9. **Conduct the second step of the second experiment.** Give the very same directions to the students as for the first part of the experiment until you come to the part about using their minds. Tell the students: *"This time while you watch your paper clip and try to keep it steady with your arm and your hand let's do a change of mind! This time you see it move and intend that it will move. Keep seeing it move in your mind and intend it to move."* (Repeat this last sentence once more slowly.)

   Pause for about 10 more seconds. In most cases the students' paper clips amazingly will gently sway. As soon as most or all of the paper clips are swaying, ask the students: *"What is your paper clip doing?"*

10. **Derive meaning by asking the students,**

    — *"Did your mind's ability to imagine and visualize have more power than your arm and hand?"*

    — *"Did you expect this to happen?"*

    — *"What does this tell you about the power of your mind and how it could be used to your advantage especially when you need to control yourself in difficult situations?"*

11. **Elaborate and challenge the students:** *"Our minds are far more powerful than we generally give them credit for. The power of our minds to create the best outcome in touchy situations by visualizing and intending those best outcomes is amazing! Just like the swaying paper clip, the things our minds 'see' and 'intend' are what tend to happen."*

    Point out: *"This is the second power we revealed to ourselves today. You can use it along with your breath to help yourself achieve self-control. KNOWING YOU CAN DO THIS IS THE KEY TO BEING ABLE TO DO IT! That's what personal power is! It's a power you had all along. You just needed to know some of the secrets for how to use it."*

12. **Direct the students to return their attention to their experience sheets.** Direct them to write their responses to questions 6 through 10. Encourage discussion among them about what happened.

13. **Summarize the knowledge these experiments provided.** Call on a student to read the "Did you know...?" segment at the beginning of the experience sheet and another one to read the two bulleted statements at the end.

You've Got the Power!

Student Experience Sheet #13

Did you know ...?

- Conscious deep breathing strengthens the power of self-control in difficult situations.
- Using your mind to visualize positive outcomes in difficult situations helps you manage your anger and make those outcomes happen.
- Awareness that you possess the personal power to control yourself and manage your anger enables you to use it.

Your teacher or counselor will lead your class through two experiments. Both experiments have two steps. All you a thread, a paper clip, curiosity, and an open mind!

First Experiment Notes:

1. Briefly describe the conditions of the first step of the first experiment:

   _____
   _____
   _____

   15"

2. What was added in the second step?

   _____
   _____
   _____

3. Did breathing deeply the second time make a difference?" Describe what happened.

_____
_____
_____
_____

4. Did you expect this to happen? _____

5. What does this tell you about how you could use your own breathing to help you in difficult situations?

_____
_____
_____
_____

Second Experiment Notes:

6. Briefly describe the conditions of the first step of the second experiment:

_____
_____
_____
_____

7. What was changed in the second step?

_____
_____

8. Did using your mind to see (visualize) and intend that the paper clip would move make a difference? Describe what happened.

_____
_____
_____
_____

9. Did you expect this to happen? _____

10. What does this tell you about how you could use the power of your mind to visualize and intend positive outcomes in difficult situations?

_____
_____
_____
_____

TWO POWERS YOU POSSESS WERE REVEALED IN THESE EXPERIMENTS: THE POWER OF YOUR BREATH AND THE POWER OF YOUR MIND.

KNOWING YOU CAN USE THEM BOTH IS THE KEY TO DOING IT WHENEVER YOU CHOOSE. THAT'S WHAT PERSONAL POWER IS--IT'S A POWER YOU HAD ALL ALONG!

Lesson 14: Be Assertive!

Purpose:

This learning activity helps students understand:

- A useful way to view human social behavior is to categorize it in these three styles: aggressive, submissive and assertive.
- The aggressive and submissive styles come from feelings of inner weakness; the assertive style comes from inner feelings of confidence and strength.
- Each style shows itself in body language and tone of voice as well as spoken words.
- The assertive style is the most desirable of the three because it fosters respect for oneself and others and leads to constructive outcomes.
- It takes self-control and anger management skills to be assertive.
- The reward for assertive self-talk and action is positive personal power!

Materials:

A copy of the Student Experience Sheet, #14, "Be Assertive!" for each student

Preparations:

Write the words, AGGRESSIVE, SUBMISSIVE and ASSERTIVE on the whiteboard for the students to see as they enter the classroom. Draw vertical lines between the terms and leave space under each one for students' statements you will ask for later.

Note:

This lesson sets the stage for the next five lessons which will focus on specific assertive strategies to help students stay in control of themselves and manage their anger in difficult situations.

Directions:

1. **Initiate the activity by pointing to the three terms.** Ask the students what they think the terms mean. Listen to a few responses but don't chart their remarks until later. (It is likely that they will have a positive feeling about the word, "Aggressive," because it is often meant to describe a successful "go-getter." Explain that in this case the word is used differently. It's used to describe a way people interact with others.)

2. **Form teams of four and distribute a copy of Student Experience Sheet, #14, "Be Assertive!" to each student.** Explain: *"I'm going to read the description of each style while you close your eyes and listen or read along silently. Focus your mind carefully on each one and how you feel about people when they are acting in each of these ways."*

3. **Read the following description aloud:**

    The Aggressive Style

    People who are aggressive with other people have a "me first" attitude that shows up in their harsh tone of voice and body posture that often invades other people's space. Many aggressive people stare other people down. They are seen as pushy, hotheads or bullies. Others can appear to be sensitive and even charming at times but in truth are not concerned with anyone's well being but their own. Aggressive people are known for not playing fair. They will take advantage of others whenever they get the chance. They frequently try to intimidate and overpower others with subtle or clearly stated threats. Sometimes they are hostile and use harsh words as well as other forms of verbal violence. Sometimes they become physically violent.

    Many people who act aggressively have been hurt by other aggressive people and actually feel weak and insecure inside. They behave aggressively as a false, protective shield and don't want anyone to know how they really feel about themselves.

4. **Ask the class:** *"How do you feel about people who act like this?"* Listen to their responses and chart their statements under the term, AGGRESSIVE.

5. **Read the following description aloud:**

    The Submissive Style

    Submissive people generally feel insecure and frequently show it by slumping, drawing back and looking away from other people and speaking in a timid voice. They are often afraid to stand up for themselves and frequently allow other people to take advantage of them. Submissive people are known to put themselves down, apologize when they should be the one apologized to, and constantly seek the approval of others.

6. **Ask the class:** *"How do you feel about people who act like this?"* Listen to their responses and chart their statements under the term, SUBMISSIVE.

7. **Read the following description aloud:**

   The Assertive Style

   Assertive people don't resort to the tactics of aggressive people, but they are not wimps or losers! This shows up in their straight posture, appropriate eye contact and even tone of voice. They control themselves well and stand up for themselves while remaining cool and calm. They are respectful, but direct, about their feelings, needs, and desires. They are confident and they know their rights. However, they know and respect the rights of others as well.

   Ask the class: *"How do you feel about people who act like this?"* Listen to their responses and chart their statements under the term, ASSERTIVE.

8. **Challenge the students to identify typical self-talk of each style and to fill in the blanks a. through m. on their experience sheets.** Point out: *"Each style has its own mind-state—the way people in each category talk to themselves. Work with your team members to see how well you can tell which one is which. Any questions?"*

Note:

Here are the "Self Talk" statements with the answers. (The experience sheets do not show the answers.)

   a. "I always get things wrong." (submissive)

   b. "I know that all individuals are equally important, including me." (assertive)

   c. "Other people are more important than me." (submissive)

   d. "My way or the highway!" (aggressive)

   e. "I know how I feel, what I need, and what I want. I can state my feelings, needs and wants to other people when I choose to." (assertive)

   f. "I must never cause anyone to be disappointed or disapprove of me." (submissive)

   g. "I should never say no to anyone for any reason." (submissive)

   h. "If I don't understand a situation I can ask questions to find out what I need to know." (assertive)

   i. "Get them before they get you. The best defense is an offense." (aggressive)

   j. "How you play doesn't count, only that you win." (aggressive)

k. "I have the right to ask for what I want, or need, and other people have the right to say yes, or no. I can't complain if I don't get what I want if I didn't ask for it." (assertive)

l. "I should never give anyone a stomach ache or headache except myself." (submissive)

m. "I'd better keep quiet and not ask questions about situations I don't understand." (submissive)

9. **Challenge the students to identify typical actions of each style and to continue filling in the blanks n. through z. on their experience sheets. Point out:** *"Each style has its own ways of behaving as well as its own types of self-talk. Work with your team members to identify the behaviors of each style."*

Note:

Here are the behavior statements with the answers. (The experience sheets do not show the answers.)

n. They permit others to hurt, humiliate, or take advantage of them. (submissive)

o. They express themselves openly and honestly to communicate their feelings, wants, and needs without demanding them. (assertive)

p. They frequently grovel and make negative statements about themselves. (submissive)

q. They intentionally attack, take advantage of, humiliate, hurt, and put other people down. (aggressive)

r. They are usually outraged if anyone treats them disrespectfully. (aggressive)

s. If someone behaves offensively toward them, they immediately give in and give way. (submissive)

t. They show respect for the feelings, wants and needs of others. They understand that individuals have a right to their own point of view. (assertive)

u. Sometimes they act covertly like gossiping, or starting rumors. (aggressive)

v. If someone behaves offensively toward them they immediately counterattack. (aggressive)

w. If someone's behavior toward them is offensive they ask what the problem is without attacking back or becoming defensive. (assertive)

x. They rarely speak up with their opinions, or ask questions about situations they don't understand. (submissive)

y. They jump to conclusions and react to situations based on assumptions that are often not correct. (aggressive)

z. They surround themselves with people they can easily control. (aggressive)

10. **After the teams have concluded filling in the blanks review their responses.** Ask if there are any answers to the statements they disagreed on. Discuss each of the ones in question, perhaps asking the class how they determined the answer. Finally, tell them your answer if need be.

11. **Direct the student's attention to the "Did you know ...?"** segment at the top of their experience sheets. Ask for readers to read them aloud to the class as a summary. Additionally, point out the final statement at the end of the experience sheet.

12. **Conclude the lesson by telling the students that assertiveness will be a big factor in the next five lessons. Explain:** *"We will learn skills of self-controll using assertive strategies in difficult, anger-provoking situations that involve other people. For the rest of today be as assertive as you can and keep it up into the future!"*

Be Assertive!

Student Experience Sheet #14

Did you know ...?

- A useful way to view human social behavior (how people interact with each other) is to categorize it in these three styles: aggressive, submissive and assertive.
- The aggressive and submissive styles come from feelings of inner weakness; the assertive style comes from inner feelings of confidence and strength.
- Each style shows itself in body language and tone of voice as well as spoken words.
- The assertive style is the most desirable of the three because it fosters respect for oneself and others and leads to constructive outcomes.
- It takes self-control and anger management skills to be assertive.
- The reward for assertive self-talk and action is positive personal power.

As you read these descriptions of how people act in each style think about how you feel about them.

The Aggressive Style

People who are aggressive with other people have a "me first" attitude that shows up in their harsh tone of voice and body posture that often invades other people's space. Many aggressive people stare other people down. They are seen as pushy, hotheads or bullies. Others can appear to be sensitive and even charming at times but in truth are not concerned with anyone's well being but their own. Aggressive people are known for not playing fair. They will take advantage of others whenever they get the chance. They frequently try to intimidate and overpower others with subtle or clearly stated threats. Sometimes they are hostile and use harsh words as well as other forms of verbal violence. Sometimes they become physically violent.

Many people who act aggressively have been hurt by other aggressive people and actually feel weak and insecure inside. They behave aggressively as a false, protective shield and don't want anyone to know how they really feel about themselves.

The Submissive Style

Submissive people generally feel insecure and frequently show it by slumping, drawing back and looking away from other people and speaking in a timid voice. They are often afraid to stand up for themselves and frequently allow other people to take advantage of them. Submissive people are known to put themselves down, apologize when they should be the one apologized to, and constantly seek the approval of others.

The Assertive Style

Assertive people don't resort to the tactics of aggressive people, but they are not wimps or losers! This shows up in their straight posture, appropriate eye contact and even tone of voice. They control themselves well and stand up for themselves while remaining cool and calm. They are respectful, but direct, about their feelings, needs, and desires. They are confident and they know their rights. However, they know and respect the rights of others as well.

Here are ways people think to themselves when they are in an aggressive, submissive or assertive style. Talk about each one with the members of your team to see if you can tell which is which.

a. "I always get things wrong." _____

b. "I know that all individuals are equally important, including me." _____

c. "Other people are more important than me." _____

d. "My way or the highway." _____

e. "I know how I feel, what I need, and what I want. I can state my feelings, needs and wants to other people when I choose to." _____

f. "I must never cause anyone to be disappointed or disapprove of me." _____

g. "I should never say no to anyone for any reason." _____

h. "If I don't understand a situation I can ask questions to find out what I need to know." _____

i. "Get them before they get you. The best defense is an offense." _____

j. "How you play doesn't count, only that you win." _____

k. "I have the right to ask for what I want, or need, and other people have the right to say yes, or no. I can't complain if I don't get what I want if I didn't ask for it." _____

l. "I should never give anyone a stomach ache or headache except myself." _____

m. "I'd better keep quiet and not ask questions about situations I don't understand." _____

Next, here are some typical actions of each style. Talk them over with the members of your team to see how well you can identify them.

n. They permit others to hurt, humiliate, or take advantage of them. _____

o. They express themselves openly and honestly to communicate their feelings, wants, and needs without demanding them. _____

p. They frequently grovel and make negative statements about themselves. _____

q. They intentionally attack, take advantage of, humiliate, hurt, and put other people down. _____

r. They are usually outraged if anyone treats them disrespectfully. _____

s. If someone behaves offensively toward them, they immediately give in and give way. _____

t. They show respect for the feelings, wants and needs of others. They understand that individuals have a right to their own point of view. _____

u. Sometimes they act covertly like gossiping, or starting rumors. _____

v. If someone behaves offensively toward them they immediately counterattack. _____

w. If someone's behavior toward them is offensive they ask what the problem is without attacking back or becoming defensive. _____

x. They rarely speak up with their opinions, or ask questions about situations they don't understand. _____

y. They jump to conclusions and react to situations based on assumptions that are often not correct. _____

z. They surround themselves with people they can easily control. _____

Keep this in mind: Your ability to think assertively and take assertive action is evidence of your personal power!

Lesson 15: Stand Up For Yourself!

Purpose:

This learning activity helps students understand:

- Sometimes it's necessary to confront people for their offensive actions. The manner in which the confrontation occurs could be constructive or destructive.
- Delivering a "You Message," is usually destructive because it blames the other person. No one likes to be blamed, even people who know they are guilty. Angry responses are likely to occur leading to an escalating, unproductive conflict.
- The use of an "I Message" is a constructive, assertive way to confront a person when it's necessary.
- Delivering an "I Message" consists of telling the offender how you feel about the offense and why, and asking him or her firmly in an even tone of voice, and respectfully, not to do it again.
- An "I Message" will have very little effect if it is not delivered with strong body language.

Materials:

A copy of the Student Experience Sheet #15, "Stand Up For Yourself!" for each student

Whiteboard with sufficient space for two side-by-side lists of students' reactions to each of your two demonstrations. (See steps 4 and 7.)

Note:

This is the first in a series of five lessons designed to help students increase their self control and develop skills for managing conflicts with assertive strategies. Lesson 14, Be Assertive! Is a valuable introduction to these five lessons.

Directions:

1. **Gain the student's attention by asking,** *"Have you ever had someone do or say something you didn't appreciate?"* Listen to, and respectfully acknowledge, their immediate reactions. Elaborate: *"Yes. Of course this has happened to us all. So what should we do--start a fight or just submissively let it keep happening without standing up for ourselves? Let's learn how to assertively respond to people when they have offended us. It's*

a conflict management strategy we can become skillful at so let's find out more about it and learn to do it well!"

2. **Set the stage for the first of two demonstrations.** Tell the students: *"There's a way that's almost always wrong and a way that's almost always right for confronting someone in this kind of situation. Let's try something. Imagine that I am your mother (or dad) confronting you about a mess you didn't clean up in the kitchen after you made yourself a snack. Listen to my message to you about the mess and notice how you feel about the message and the way I say it."*

3. **Deliver the "You Message" with a critical tone:**

   "You left a huge mess in the kitchen again! You have no consideration for the other people in this family. You just do what you want and too bad for everyone else. What's wrong with you?"

4. **Evaluate the "You Message."** Ask: *"How did you feel about what I said?"* Listen to, and chart, the students' responses on one side of the whiteboard. They will probably state that they felt blamed and attacked. After you have charted several reactions, write YOU MESSAGE over the students' statements.

5. **Set the stage for the second demonstration.** Tell the students: *"There will now be a replay of the very same situation, but with a variation in my words and tone. Notice how you feel about this message."*

6. **Deliver the "I Message" with an even tone.**

   "I feel disappointed and upset that you left a mess in the kitchen after your snack because I had just cleaned it up. I'd like for you to remember to clean up your mess after you use the kitchen from now on. What do you say?"

7. **Evaluate the "I Message."** Ask: *"How did you feel about what I said that time?"* As before, chart the students' responses to this question on the other side of the whiteboard. They will probably state that they didn't feel so put down and more likely to remember to clean up their mess next time. (Don't write I MESSAGE over the students' statements just yet.)

8. **Ask the key question: "What did I do that was different the second time?"**

9. **Help the students identify what was different the second time.** If they don't recognize that you began each sentence with the word, "I" give them a hint: *"In the first demonstration I began each sentence, except for one, with the word, 'you,' which is perfect for blaming. The second time I began each sentence with a different word. What was it?"* If necessary, repeat the I Message. As soon as the students realize that you began each sentence with the word "I," write I MESSAGE over the statements you charted about the second demonstration.

10. **Help the students fully understand the impact of the two different messages.** Explain: *"The first message was a 'You Message.' I blamed and accused you several times by saying, 'you' this and 'you' that. With a critical tone I started each sentence, except for one, with the word, 'you.' People who have the skills to avoid unnecessary conflicts, and to easily and quickly settle conflicts they are in, never or rarely deliver 'You Messages' because they know that it will make the other person feel angry and up for a fight. They know that even if the person they deliver a 'You Message' to doesn't say anything back at that moment they are likely to try to get even later in some way.*

    "The second message was an 'I Message.' I told you how I felt about your leaving the kitchen in a mess and I told you why. I started each sentence, except for one, with the word, 'I,' instead of 'you.'

    "It takes courage to use an 'I Message' because when you do it you are talking about yourself--your feelings and your wishes. You aren't dumping blame on someone else. Using an 'I message' is a smart way to talk to people when you are annoyed about something they've done. With an 'I Message' you express your own feelings and concerns. In order to express them, you have to be honest with yourself and recognize what your feelings and concerns are.

    "This is a clear way to tell people how you feel and what you want and need from them without causing them to want to fight or get even. Assertive people with personal power use this strategy."

11. **Distribute Student Experience Sheet #15, "Stand Up For Yourself" to each student.**

12. **Challenge the students to use their experience sheet to develop an I Message of their own.** Explain: *"Read through the information about I Messages then use the I Message formula to write your own I Message. Think about a situation where someone hasn't done something you reasonably expected them to do or has done something that was unacceptable. Maybe you loaned something to a friend and she hasn't returned it. Perhaps someone makes insulting remarks to you and you want him to quit doing that. Use the formula to write in the whole message without writing the name of the person you are writing it to. Then be ready to share it with a partner. Go!"* Provide enough time for the students to complete their I Messages. Offer help where needed.

13. **Form partners for four steps of role playing.** When the students have finished writing and as soon as they are facing their partners facilitate a four step process as follows:

Step 1:

- "Decide who will talk first (A) and who will talk next (B).

- "A, tell B what the situation is and how it affects you without naming the person involved.

- "A, read the I Message you've written to B.

- "B, tell A your reaction as well as suggestions."

Step 2:

Reverse the process where B shares his or her situation and reads his or her I Message to A. Then A tells his or her reaction as well as suggestions.

(Steps 3 and 4 are repeats of steps 1 and 2 with direct speaking and solid body language instead of simply reading.)

Step 3:

Clue the students about body language: *"This time let's make it real! Instead of reading what you wrote pretend that your partner is the person who you need to confront with your I Message.' Use solid 'body language!' Breathe deeply. Hold your shoulders back, look your partner in the eye and deliver the message firmly in an even tone of voice and with respect."* A talks first.

Step 4:

B shares his or her I Message with solid body language.

14. **Direct the students to follow the directions for writing another I Message for a different situation as shown on the experience sheet.** When they have completed writing direct them through the four steps as you did before to rehearse giving their second I Messages about other situations with their partners. Remind them to give each other feedback on their deliveries.

15. **Point out the "Let's review ..." segment at the end of the experience sheet and read it together.**

16. **Conclude with this challenge:** *"Now you have the formula for assertively dealing with tough situations in which someone has offended you in some way by what he or she has done or not done. From now on don't aggressively chew their heads off, or submissively wimp out, assertively confront them with an 'I Message!'"*

Stand Up For Yourself!

Student Experience Sheet #15

There are times when it's tempting to be aggressive and other times it seems easiest to be submissive but neither of these gives you personal power and self respect like assertiveness does. You may want to have personal power and self respect but being assertive can seem hard when someone has disappointed or offended you.

- Maybe your friend borrowed something from you but he never gave it back.
- It could be that you told someone a secret and asked her to keep it confidential but she told it to other people.
- Perhaps someone you'd always trusted made you a promise then broke it.
- Maybe someone told you a lie.

What do you do? What do you say?

These are the right questions to ask. Let's look at one assertive way to confront people who have disappointed or offended you. It's a strategy called "using an I Message."

I MESSAGE FORMULA

1. "**I FEEL** (name your true feeling(s). Don't say 'that you' after the word 'feel') **...**
2. **WHEN YOU ...**
3. **BECAUSE... .**"
4. "**WHAT I NEED FROM YOU IS** (or want or hope you will do, or stop doing, from now on) **... .**"

When you deliver an I Message to individuals who you need to stand up to, begin by telling them your feelings (Step 1) about what they did, or didn't do, or said (Step 2). Next (Step 3), tell them why you didn't appreciate it. Last (Step 4), tell them what you prefer they do, or stop doing, in the future.

Instead of delivering a YOU MESSAGE where almost every sentence begins with the word "you," almost every sentence in an I MESSAGE begins with the word "I." Not only that, body language, eye contact and tone of voice need to be assertive or it will have very little effect.

Let's look at an example:

"I'm frustrated, Brad, when you keep forgetting to return my DVD because I've been telling you how much I want to play it for my cousin. I want you to bring it to me tomorrow, okay?"

Give it a try. Here are some guidelines for writing your own I Message to someone (nameless) who you need to confront:

"I feel (name the feeling) … _____

when you … _____

_____

_____

because… _____

_____

_____.

From now on, please… _____

_____

_____."

Writing an I Message gets you off to a good start but practicing it out loud makes it real! As you say the words you've written be assertive with your body language. Stand tall, breathe deeply, look the person in the eye, speak firmly in an even tone and with respect.

Write another I Message for another person you need to confront:

"I feel (name the feeling) … _____

when you … _____

_____

_____

because… _____

_____

_____.

From now on, please… _____

_____

_____."

Let's review …

- Sometimes it's necessary to confront people for their offensive actions. The manner in which the confrontation occurs could be constructive or destructive.
- Delivering a "You Message," is usually destructive because it blames the other person. No one likes to be blamed, even people who know they are guilty. Angry responses are likely to occur leading to an escalating unproductive conflict.
- The use of an "I Message" is a constructive, assertive way to confront a person when it's necessary.
- Delivering an "I Message" consists of telling the offender how you feel about the offense and why, and asking him or her firmly in an even voice, and respectfully, not to do it again.
- An "I Message" will have very little effect if it is not delivered with strong body language.

Give it a try in "real life" and see what happens!

Lesson 16: Assertive Conflict Management Strategies that Work!

Purpose:

This learning activity helps students gain understanding and skills as follows:

- Conflicts arise in all of our lives. When they do we can respond in aggressive, submissive or assertive ways.
- Three strategies, "Listen to Understand," "Compromising," and "Apologizing and/or Expressing Regret" are assertive and constructive ways to manage conflicts.
- Respectful body language, appropriate eye contact and an even tone of voice are necessary when using all of the strategies, especially, "Listen to Understand."
- Self control to remain silent and patient until a person who's upset finishes talking is the key to "Listen to Understand."
- Compromising works when the person who suggests it is willing to be the first to give up part of what they both want.
- A sincere apology and/or an expression of regret can be an amazingly strong conflict management strategy when you have offended someone (or the person thinks you have done or said something offensive).

Materials:

A copy of the Student Experience Sheet #16, "Assertive Conflict Management Strategies that Work" for each student

Preparations:

Write the names of these assertive conflict management strategies on the whiteboard for the students to see as they enter the classroom:

        LISTEN TO UNDERSTAND   COMPROMISING

        APOLOGIZING AND/OR EXPRESSING REGRET.

Directions:

1. **Begin the activity with a review of "I Messages" from Lesson #15.** Ask the class: *"Has anyone tried using an 'I Message' since our lesson about how it works? Without naming names, tell us what happened and how you formed the message. Also, tell us how it worked out for you."* Listen to the students' responses and acknowledge their attempts to use the strategy.

   (It is likely that the students encountered some resistance in the people they addressed. If this occurred, explain: *"Sometimes someone will ask you what you are up to. They know you're doing something different and they act like you're being weird. That's natural. It happens a lot when you first start using a strategy like 'I Messages.' But don't let that stop you. Just keep it up. Eventually they will realize you mean business and stop testing you."*

2. **Point to the whiteboard and tell the students:** "***There are several more strategies we will learn how to use.*** *Today we will focus on three more. They are 'listen to understand,' 'compromising' and 'apologizing and/or expressing regret.'"*

3. **Describe how "Listen to Understand" works:** *"'Listen to Understand' is a strategy to use when you find yourself in an argument. Have you noticed how you feel when you are upset about something and the other person, or people, won't listen? It just makes things worse. But if the other person listens to your feelings it can change an argument into a sensible conversation.*

   "Probably the best way to settle a tense situation with someone is to use this strategy. When you do it you start by changing your focus from figuring out what you're going to say to trying to understand what the other person is saying, and especially what the person is feeling. So you just stop talking and start listening. To do it right you have to be respectful, sincere and silent no matter how much you want to speak. When you use 'Listen to Understand' you lean forward, look into the person's eyes, and really try to understand him or her, especially his or her feelings and opinions. You keep a pleasant, respectful expression on your face while you continue listening. At some point he or she will finally be ready to listen to you. But it may be awhile so be very patient.

   "When the person wants to know what you have to say start out with empathy. You might say something like, 'I can see how serious you are about this. ...' 'You feel ... ' 'You think ...' Check to see if the person agrees or not. If not, listen some more until the person is through talking. Check again to see if you understand. Then simply agree with what the other person has stated or if you see things differently you might start out by saying, 'Here's the way I look at it ... .' Perhaps the person is upset because of something you did to cause offense. If so, apologize. It's

possible you will be interrupted. Stay in control of yourself if this happens. As before, let the person speak until he or she has finished.

"You may think that this strategy, 'Listen to Understand,' weakens your position, but guess again. If you stay in control of yourself and really try to understand how the person is feeling, it strengthens you and keeps the situation from escalating into an unnecessary destructive conflict."

4. **Form partners for role playing "Listen to Understand."** As soon as the students are facing their partners ask them to decide who will be the one to talk and who will be the one to use "Listen to Understand." Suggest that the speaker complain non-stop about something they are pretending the listener did. Remind the students that this is a practice in listening, not speaking. Advise the students that they have two minutes to listen to the speaker without saying a word and to pretend that the speaker has already been complaining for a long time. At the end of the two minutes, direct them to switch roles. Give them two more minutes for the second speaker to talk.

5. **Debrief. Ask the students:**

   — *"How did it feel to be the listener? Was it difficult to keep silent?"*

   — *"How did it feel to be the speaker when your listener just listened and said nothing?"*

6. **Help the students grasp the value of "Listen to Understand."** Explain: *"Angry energy is pumped up in an argument when both people attack each other with hostile words and facial expressions. But when one person simply remains respectfully silent it generally reduces the other person's angry energy. This usually allows for a peaceful settlement of the conflict."*

7. **Point out that verbal abuse is another matter.** State: *"No one deserves to be abused physically or verbally. The best thing to do is to get away from someone who is 'beating you up verbally' by threatening you, swearing at you, or calling you very bad names. Leave as soon and as smoothly as you can without causing more hostility."*

8. **Describe how "Compromising" works:** *"Let's say an impossible situation has presented itself: You and another person both want the same thing at the same time. So you suggest a compromise that allows each of you to get some of it. You could share something like a sandwich, or take turns using something like a laptop. The way you use this strategy is to offer to give up something if the other person will do the same. The key is that you make the offer and you show that you will give up some of your part first. This almost always causes the other person to agree to cooperate. If the thing you both want can't be divided or if the other person refuses to compromise, suggest flipping a coin."*

9. **Ask the students to suggest situations where compromise could be used for their next role play. Situations could include:**

   - Two family members want to watch different movies on TV at the same time.

   - Two people want the same seat on the bleachers.

   - Two siblings want their mom to drive them to two different places at the same time.

   - Two children you are babysitting want a candy bar you brought to their house.

10. **Direct the partners to role play "Compromising."** First they should be given a minute to decide on the situation they want to role play. Then give them one minute to role play the first segment. One student should be argumentative and the other suggests the compromise. Roles are reversed for a second minute.

11. **Debrief. Ask the students:**

   — *"How did it feel to be the one to suggest compromising?"*

   — *"How did it work out?"*

12. **Describe how "Apologizing and/or Expressing Regret" works:**
    Explain: *"These can be hard ones for some people because they think they are being weak or that they are admitting they did something harmful on purpose when maybe it isn't so. It may feel awkward but in many cases a sincere apology and admitting your mistake, if you in fact made one, is the best strategy. Remember, everyone has a right to their feelings even when the feeling is anger and it's directed at you!*

    "There are also times when you didn't say, or do, exactly what they think you said, or did. Let's suppose you say something and someone takes it the wrong way. Tell the person so as soon as you realize he or she is hurt or angry. Then have the strength to say you're sorry and explain that you never meant to cause bad feelings.

    "Accidents are another example. You may have caused an accident somehow, but not on purpose. That's when you might prefer to express regret. You could say, 'It's terrible that it happened. I don't blame you for being mad' or 'I regret that I ...' 'I didn't do it on purpose. Here, let me help.' When other people know you feel regret, and that you care about them, in almost every case it takes away their upset feelings."

13. **Direct the partners to role play "Apologizing and/or Expressing Regret."** Give the students a minute to imagine something one might have done to offend the other. Then give them two one-minute segments

allowing each partner to take a turn to apologize and/or express regret to the other for the imaginary offense.

14. **Debrief. Ask the students:**

    — *"How did it feel to apologize and/or express regret? Did it seem to have an effect on your partner?"*

    — *"When you were apologized to, or received an expression of regret, how did it feel?"*

15. **Distribute Student Experience Sheet #16, "Assertive Conflict Management Strategies that Work!"** Ask the students to read it with their partners. It serves as a review of the three strategies offered in this lesson. It also offers them a chance to write about a time when they may have used one of these strategies.

    (The experience sheet for Lesson #17, "More Assertive Conflict Management Strategies that Work!" will offer a variety of conflict situations that challenge the students to decide which strategy or combination of strategies would work best in each situation.)

16. **Call on a student to read the "Let's Review..." segment aloud.**

17. **Close with this statement:** *"Now you have three more strategies you can use to manage conflicts. Over the next few days remember them. They might come in handy!"*

Assertive Conflict Management Strategies that Work!

Student Experience Sheet #16

Here are three more assertive and constructive conflict management strategies. You are in a powerful position when you remember these strategies and use them with self control when a conflict occurs. Using these strategies can also increase your self respect and personal power!

Let's take a look at the three strategies:

Listen to Understand

Use this strategy when you find yourself in an argument. No doubt you've noticed how you feel when you are trying to get your thoughts across to another person and he or she won't listen to you.

When you use the strategy, Listen to Understand, you focus on the other person not on what you want to say next. You listen with eye contact and a respectful expression on your face until the person has finally finished speaking. This takes patience and lots of it because many people can go on for a very long time.

When the other person finally wants to hear what you have to say start out in an even tone of voice. Check to see if you have understood his or her feelings and opinions. Showing empathy like this usually causes the other person to settle down and listen to you. If the other person interrupts you go along with it and listen some more. Keep this up until you either have reached a point where you have settled the argument or agreed to put it off for another time. When you use this strategy it may seem like you are giving in a lot but *the truth is that you have been in full control of yourself and the conflict.*

Compromising

This strategy works when two or more people or groups want the same thing at the same time. When you find yourself in such a situation and you want to take positive control, you suggest a compromise that allows each of you to get some of it. You could share something, or take turns using something. The way you use this strategy is to offer to give up something if the other person will do the same. *The key is that you make the offer and you show that you will give up some of your part first.* This almost always causes the other person to agree to cooperate. If the thing you both want can't be divided or if the other person refuses to compromise, suggest flipping a coin. Once again, you are the one who's in control of yourself and the outcome of the conflict.

Apologizing and/or Expressing Regret

Saying, "I'm sorry" is hard for some people because they feel they are showing weakness. But think about how you feel when someone has offended you and won't apologize. *It actually shows strength to be able to admit it when you've made a mistake and hurt someone in some way.* That's when apologizing is the right and strong thing to do. But sometimes it doesn't seem right to apologize because what happened as a result of something you said or did was something you didn't mean to say or do. That's when expressing regret may be best. *The main idea is that you show the other person or people that you care about them.* This has a way of calming everyone down. Your own self control, honesty and courage to do the right thing earns you respect from others and your own self respect as well.

Have you used any of these strategies successfully? Write a short story about one situation and how your use of the strategy helped to resolve the conflict.

_____
_____
_____
_____
_____
_____
_____
_____
_____
_____

Let's review ...

- Conflicts arise in all of our lives. When they do we can respond in aggressive, submissive or assertive ways.

- Three strategies, "Listen to Understand," "Compromising," and "Apologizing and/or Expressing Regret" are assertive and constructive ways to manage conflicts.

- Respectful body language, appropriate eye contact and an even tone of voice are necessary when using all of the strategies, especially Listen to Understand.

- Self control to remain silent and patient until a person who's upset finishes talking is the key to Listen to Understand.

- Compromising works when the person who suggests it is willing to give up part of what they both want first.

- A sincere apology and/or an expression of regret can be an amazingly strong conflict management strategy when you have offended someone (or the person thinks you have done or said something offensive).

Lesson 17: More Assertive Conflict Management Strategies that Work!

Purpose:

This learning activity helps students gain understanding and skills as follows:

- Conflicts arise in all of our lives. When they do we can respond in aggressive, submissive or assertive ways.
- Two additional strategies, "Postponing," and "Problem Solving," are assertive and constructive ways to manage conflicts.
- Respectful body language, appropriate eye contact and an even tone of voice are necessary when using all of the strategies.
- Self control to determine that conditions are not good for trying to resolve a conflict *right now* is the key to postponing.
- Self control to understand how unhelpful it is to blame another person for a problem, and withholding blame, are the keys to successful problem solving.
- Problem solving is an agreed upon combination of specific assertive conflict management strategies used to solve a problem.
- Problem solving is best accomplished when the people involved take the attitude: "It's you and me against the problem, not me against you."

Materials:

A copy of the Student Experience Sheet #17, "More Assertive Conflict Management Strategies that Work" for each student

Preparations:

Write the names of these assertive conflict management strategies on the whiteboard for the students to see as they enter the classroom: POSTPONING and PROBLEM SOLVING.

Directions:

1. **Begin the activity by reviewing "Listen to Understand," "Compromising," and "Apologizing and/or Expressing Regret."** Ask the class, *"Has anyone tried using one or more of the three strategies we role played in our last lesson? If you've tried one tell us what happened without saying the names of the other person, or people, who were*

involved." Listen to the students' responses and acknowledge their attempts to use the strategies.

2. **Announce the focus for today's lesson.** Point to the whiteboard and tell the students: *"Today we will learn how to use two more strategies. They are '"Postponing," and "Problem Solving."*

3. **Describe how "Postponing" works:** *"Have you ever noticed how stupid and ugly fights can get when one, or both, people are in a bad mood, hungry, or tired? The strategy of postponing is exactly that--you suggest that you put off discussing the matter and get back to it later. You could say, 'Hey, I've had a long day and I feel lousy. Could we get back to this tomorrow?' or 'I've got an idea. Let's go eat and talk about this afterward. I'm so starved I can't think straight. What about you?' Do be sure to get back with the person later at the agreed-upon time and then start out with 'Listen to Understand.' In other cases you both might decide to let the whole matter drop."*

4. **Brainstorm ideas for topics partners could "argue" about.** Before forming partners, ask the class to come up with some "argument topics" they could use for role playing an argument that needs to be postponed because one or both of the "arguers" are hungry, tired or just in a bad mood. Almost any topic that two people could disagree on will work.

5. **Form partners as soon as a number of ideas for "argument topics" have been generated.** When the partners are facing each other direct them to decide who will be the first one to suggest postponing after one minute of arguing. Then give them a minute for the first segment. At the end of the minute tell them to reverse roles for a second one-minute segment.

6. **Debrief.** Ask the students how it went and listen to their responses. Point out that when someone is very upset and can't stop complaining, they are not able to hear a word said to them. That might be a signal to suggest "postponing."

7. **Describe how "Problem Solving" works:** *"Sometimes things can get complicated between you and another person or group. With the strategy of problem solving you use as many of the other strategies as you can especially 'Listen to Understand.' If you don't understand the other person, don't interrupt. When he or she finishes talking, explain in a calm, respectful tone of voice that you don't understand and ask questions. Then listen some more. Next, see if you can define the problem without any blaming. Take the attitude that the two of you are against the problem, not against each other. Suggest brainstorming ideas for solutions to the problem together and then agree on one, or more, that seems to make the*

most sense. Compromising might be one of the strategies you will need to use. If you can't agree on a solution, postpone deciding until later after each of you has had a chance to calm down and think about it some more."

8. **Ask the class to brainstorm some typical, yet somewhat complicated, problems they have faced, or are facing.** The list could include:

   - Your parent wants you to observe a curfew that you think is unfair.

   - Your friend wants you to join a club he or she is about to join, but you have another club in mind and want your friend to join it.

   - Your mom says you can have a holiday party but each of you has different ideas about the date and whether it should be held at your home or somewhere else.

9. **Direct the students to take a minute as partners to plan their "problem solving" role play.** Ask them to select a problem they want to try to solve together in a role play and which one should take each role. Explain: *"One partner should be "difficult"—blaming, irritable and hopeless about solving the problem. The other partner should role play the attitude of 'It's me and you against the problem, not me against you.' That partner should listen respectfully and suggest at least two strategies for solving the problem."* Give the partners two minutes each, taking turns to role play each role.

10. **Ask the students how it feels to use the strategies they have learned to try to solve a problem.** Listen to their responses and acknowledge their efforts.

11. **Distribute Student Experience Sheet #17, "More Assertive Conflict Management Strategies that Work."** Challenge the students to read all of it with their partners and to respond to the questions about what strategy or strategies would work best in a variety of conflict situations that are presented. The six strategies are listed in the experience sheet.

12. ***Discuss the students' responses to the situations offered in the experience sheet as soon as they have completed discussing them.*** *"Here are the answers: (1) compromise, (2) I message, (3) apologize and express regret, (4) I message, (5) listen to understand and apologize and/or express regret, (6) problem solve, (7) compromise, (8) listen to understand and apologize and/or express regret, (9) postpone, (10) problem solve, (11) apologize and express regret, (12) postpone, (13) I message."*

13. ***Congratulate and challenge the students:*** *"You have succeeded in learning about how to use six strategies for managing conflicts assertively and constructively. But this is just the beginning. Now you can use them in your life. When difficult situations come up, take charge and get control of yourself. Then think about which strategy, or strategies, might work best. Go for it and see what happens!"*

More Assertive Conflict Management Strategies that Work!

Student Experience Sheet #17

Here are two more assertive and constructive conflict management strategies. Let's take a look at them.

Postponing

Have you ever noticed how fights usually happen when one, or both, people are in a bad mood, hungry, or tired? *The strategy of postponing is exactly that--you suggest putting off discussing the matter and getting back to it later.* You could say, "You know, if I don't eat something pretty soon I don't know what I'll do. I missed lunch and its way past dinner time. Let's eat and then get back to this afterward, okay?" or "I'm not at my best right now. I had a hard day and I need to chill. Let's let this go until tomorrow. Are you okay with that?" Keep this in mind too: It's important in many cases not to forget to reconnect when you said you would. In other cases you both might decide to let the whole matter drop.

Problem Solving

This strategy works best when a complicated problem has come up between you and someone else or a group. With the strategy of problem solving you combine the use of some of the other strategies that might help. Listen to Understand is often a good strategy for starters. Then maybe there needs to be a compromise or if one person or more has a need like resting or eating, postponing might help. For problem solving to work well everyone involved needs to understand the full extent of the problem and be willing to help solve it. Brainstorming possible solutions sometimes helps. Asking questions is also a good idea. *It's important to have a "no blame, no gain" agreement.* Rather, it works best if everyone involved has the attitude: "It's not me against you—it's you and me against the problem."

You have been learning how to use six assertive conflict management strategies. They are:

- I Messages
- Listen to Understand
- Compromising
- Apologizing and/or Expressing Regret
- Postponing
- Problem Solving

Imagine that you find yourself in these conflict situations. What strategy or strategies might work in each case?

1. Jude is on a soccer team. He plays forward well and so do two other boys. Their coach can't come to their next game to make decisions and all three want to play forward. They have to work this problem out for themselves. Jude remembers a strategy from class to solve the problem. What do you think it is?

   _____

2. Sandy is aggravated with Jannelle because she loaned her a hoodie she really likes. Jannelle hasn't returned it after Sandy's asked twice for her to give it back. What should Sandy do now?

   _____

3. Jannelle borrowed Sandy's hoodie and then she lost it. Jannelle should...

___

4. Julio invites Cheryl over to his house to hang out for the afternoon. Shortly after she arrives he starts to play video games on his laptop. He asks her to watch but she's totally bored. Not only that, she's starting to feel very annoyed. What should she say to Julio?

___

5. Emma is visiting her aunt and uncle and their children, her younger cousins. After dinner she goes outside with the children who beg her to take them to the park across the busy street. Emma says okay and off they go. She's careful to get them across the street safely. After awhile her uncle comes over to the park yelling because he didn't give his permission for them to go there. Emma apologizes but all the way back he criticizes her and just keeps complaining. What should Emma do?

___

6. David is a member of a project team in his science class. Most of the other teams have begun working on their projects but his team can't even decide what to do. David is starting to get nervous about the delay. What would you suggest he do?

___

7. John's dad has a golf cart that seats him and three other people. Beside himself, John is the only other person his dad will let drive the golf cart. One evening John has six players on his baseball team over for dinner. All of them want to go for a ride in the golf cart and John's dad says sure. Then he points out that dinner will be in about half an hour and he plans to go to a meeting right after dinner. If you were John and you wanted all of your friends to get a ride in the golf cart what would you do?

___

8. Jerry's mom rants sometimes when there's too many stresses in her life. Now she's going on and on about how Jerry and his brothers are driving her nuts. Jerry should...

___

9. Margo and Tommy are friends. They're planning a party for Tommy's birthday but are having a ridiculous dispute about the cake—what kind?—how big?—what flavor for the frosting? The fact is that they are both very hungry. They should...

___

10. Tatiana's older sister is getting married. She's having a party with her bridesmaids to get their ideas for the wedding. Tatiana will be a bridesmaid too and she has some ideas of her own but she gets frustrated when all the other bridesmaids start to disagree with each other about dresses, flowers, hats—you name it. Tatiana's sister seems to be getting frustrated too. Tatiana wishes her sister would try one of the conflict management strategies she told her about. What do you think it is?

___

11. Brian is trying to get all of his books into his backpack. One slips and lands on Michelle's toe. Michelle is wearing sandals. She yelps! What should Brian do?

___

12. Elena has had a long day and a lot of homework that she's almost finished when her brother, Gilberto, walks in and tells her he's mad at her for telling a girl, Darlene, that he likes her. Elena is exhausted. She's in no mood to explain that Darlene told her she sort of likes Gilberto but only if he likes her. Perhaps she should...

___

13. Rachel and Lawrence are brother and sister. They love each other but, like many siblings, get on each other's nerves at times. Lawrence is playing music Rachel doesn't like. She approaches him planning on using one of the strategies. Which one do you think it is?

___

Let's review ...

- Using self control to determine that conditions are not good for trying to resolve a conflict *right now* is the key to postponing.

- Using self control to understand how unhelpful it is to blame another person for a problem, and withholding blame, are the keys to successful problem solving.

- Problem solving is an agreed upon combination of specific assertive conflict management strategies used to solve a problem.

- Problem solving is best accomplished when the people involved take the attitude: "It's you and me against the problem, not me against you."

Lesson 18: Don't Cave to the Pressure!

Purpose:

This learning activity helps students understand:

- People who pressure others to do something that could get them in trouble do it because they don't want to be all by themselves.
- People who pressure others in this way generally don't care about the health and safety of those others. Rather, they are taking advantage of them.
- There are a variety of useful strategies that can be used when you are a target of peer pressure.
- Other students can be a good source of ideas for what to do in a peer pressure situation.

Materials:

A copy of the Student Experience Sheet #18, "Don't Cave to the Pressure!" for each student

Directions:

1. **Initiate the activity by asking the class about peer pressure:** *"What term is frequently used when someone wants you to do something undesirable? They try to get you to do it even if you object because you don't think it's right, legal or safe?"* The students will likely respond with: "Peer Pressure."

2. **Write "Peer Pressure" on the whiteboard. Continue:** *"Right you are! And it's a tight spot to be in. Sometimes it's just one person your own age and sometimes it's older teens or even adults. Whoever it might be, it's normal to feel uncomfortable, threatened, scared, and angry when this kind of pressure occurs."*

3. **State the plan for the lesson:** *"Today we are going to share our concerns about peer pressure and share our suggestions as well. There are good ideas in this room. They're in your heads."*

4. **Form teams of four and tell a story of your own.** As soon as the teams are settled, tell the students about a peer pressure situation you experienced when you were their age that you would be comfortable sharing. Describe the feelings you experienced and what you did to extricate yourself from the situation.

5. **Distribute Student Experience Sheet #18, "Don't Cave to the Pressure."** Ask them to read the "Did you know... ?" section at the top to themselves as you read it aloud. Then ask for their questions and comments about the four points. The rest of the lesson closely follows the points offered in the experience sheet.

6. **Read the three examples of peer pressure offered as the students read them silently.** Ask them if they can add any other examples. Listen to their descriptions, then ask them to write these additional situations in the space provided.

7. **Next, focus on the ideas for getting out of these kinds of tight spots.** Read the three ideas aloud as the students read them silently. Ask them if they can add any other ideas. Listen to their suggestions then ask them to write these additional ideas for freeing themselves from the pressure in the space provided.

8. **Initiate team sharing and offering of individualized suggestions.** Ask: *"Is there a peer pressure situation that's happening to you now or that you think may happen in the future? If you have a situation you'd feel comfortable telling your team members about, you may do that now. After each team member who wishes to speak to the topic has spoken, write down what you shared on your experience sheet. Then pass your experience sheets around so that each of your team members can write an idea for you to consider trying. If you don't describe a situation of your own, you can still write suggestions for your other team members. You will have _____ minutes to do the talking and writing. Any questions?"*

9. **Notify the students about the time.** When a few minutes remain, let the students know. Encourage them to make sure each team member gets a turn to be the focus of attention.

10. **Conclude with hearing each team's best ideas.** Ask the students, *"Who would be comfortable telling all of us about the pressuring situation you told your team about and the suggestions you got from your team members for how to respond to it."* Listen to the students' contributions.

11. **Acknowledge the students for their honesty and good ideas.** Encourage them to remember all of their self-control and anger management skills as well as the suggestions they heard in class today whenever they find themselves the object of peer pressure.

Don't Cave to the Pressure!

Student Experience Sheet #18

Did you know ...?
- People who pressure others to do something that could get them in trouble do it because they don't want to be all by themselves.
- People who pressure others in this way generally don't care about the health and safety of those others. Rather, they are taking advantage of them.
- There are a variety of useful strategies that can be used when you are a target of peer pressure.
- Other students can be a good source of ideas for what to do in a peer pressure situation.

Sometimes it's a peer—someone your own age—or an older teen, or even an adult. Whoever it is, you're in an uncomfortable position if they want you to do something you know isn't wise. When this happens it's normal to feel threatened, scared and angry.

Here are some examples of peer pressure:
- A student asks you to help steal another student's IPhone as a prank.
- A 21 year old adult asks a 14-year old to go out.
- An older student wants you to "experience" a narcotic high.
- A friend wants you to ask another student an embarrassing personal question.
- A drunk adult wants you to go for a ride with him.
- Another student asks you to let her peek at your answers on a test.

Here's a space for writing down more situations that come to mind:

_____
_____
_____
_____
_____

Here are some ideas for getting yourself out of these kinds of tight spots:

- Give an excuse. (It's okay to exaggerate.) Example: "Oh no, my parents will kill me if they found out about it. I can't risk it." Then change the subject or depart.
- Turn it into a joke. Example: "You gotta be kidding me! That's the best recipe for disaster I've heard in a long time." (Laugh as you say it.) Then start a new conversation about something else or walk off.
- Be assertive and firmly say no. Example: "Thanks, but no thanks. I'd rather not!" Then shift the focus to another topic or leave.

Here's a space for writing down more ideas for ways to turn down the one who's pressuring you:

_____
_____
_____
_____
_____

Is there a peer pressure situation that's happening to you now or that you think may happen in the future? Here's a space for writing down a brief description of something you would feel comfortable talking about and having other people read:

_____
_____
_____
_____
_____
_____
_____

Give this experience sheet to your teammates to pass around and write suggestions for handling the peer pressure situation you just described.

Here's a space for their suggestions:

_____
_____
_____
_____
_____
_____
_____

Remember! You can use all of the self-control and anger management skills you've been learning as well as the suggestions you received from your team members whenever you find yourself the object of peer pressure.

Lesson 19: How to Respond to Bullying Behavior

Purpose:

This learning activity helps students understand that:

- No one is born a bully; their actions have become a set of learned destructive behaviors and habits.
- People who behave like bullies try to fool others and themselves into thinking they are strong when, in fact, their behavior is a cover up for inner feelings of weakness and vulnerability.
- Bullying behaviors come from the urge to hurt others because these people have been hurt or imagine they have been hurt. They believe that hurting others is a way to settle the score.
- Many of these people believe the world is out to get them making it their right to get what they want however they can.
- These people and their victims need genuine caring and kindness.
- Self-control and anger management skills are helpful in dealing with people who bully others and for them in dealing with themselves.

Materials:

A copy of the Student Experience Sheet #19, "How to Respond to Bullying Behavior" for each student

Directions:

1. **Initiate this lesson by telling the students a personal story.** Relay an experience you would feel comfortable sharing that you had when you were the age of your students when you were a target of bullying behavior. (If you have no personal story, borrow one you've heard.) If it's your story, describe the feelings you experienced and how you responded to the person. Answer questions the students will no doubt have for you.

2. **Ask, "*What goes on inside a person who is acting like a bully?*"** Explain, *"That will be our focus today. Also, we will talk about what to do if you become the target of bullying behavior. The main idea is to stay safe."*

3. **Distribute Student Experience Sheet #19, "How to Respond to Bullying Behavior."** Ask the students to close their eyes and listen or read along silently as you read the opening essay aloud, "What Do People Who Act Like Bullies Want?" from the student experience sheet. When you come to the specific suggestions, you may wish to have students take turns reading them aloud.

4. **Form teams of four allowing students to tell each other about bullying experiences.** Tell the students: *"Your topic is to describe a time you were bullied that you would feel comfortable sharing. Without mentioning names tell your team members what happened and how you felt at the time. Another thing: if you used any of the ideas in the essay tell how you used them and how they worked. If you used another strategy tell about it and how it worked. Let each person have a turn to talk before you ask each other questions."*

5. **Assign the first writing activity.** After the teams have finished sharing, explain: *"Next, write a brief description of what happened in your story about a time you were bullied in the space on your experience sheet. Keep it to just a few sentences and take about _____ minutes."*

6. **Assign the second writing activity.** Explain, *"While you were listening to the incidents the other members of your team told about you probably thought of ways to respond to the people in those stories besides the ones listed in the essay. Let's find out what those ideas might be. Pass your experience sheets to the other members of your team and write in ideas for each other that might have worked in the situations each of you told about. Let's take about _____ minutes for this. I will be visiting the teams and will be available if you have any questions."*

7. **Conclude by directing the teams to read the "Let's review... " segment at the end of their experience sheets.** Encourage them to remember the ideas they heard today if they should be the target of bullying behavior in the future.

How to Respond to Bullying Behavior

Student Experience Sheet #19

Essay: What Do People Who Behave Like Bullies Want?

People who act like bullies want respect but will settle for attention, control, or fear. They may seem strong and scary but it's all an act. They are trying to convince you that they could do you damage, but mainly they are trying to convince themselves. Inside, they feel anything but strong but by controlling, scaring, and hurting other people they fool themselves into thinking they are proving their strength.

These people act like they can damage you because they have been damaged or imagine they have been damaged. They may have been victims of bad treatment probably as small children. Many were abused and may not remember it. Some still live with abusive people in their homes or neighborhoods. Being hurt, or imagining they have been hurt, causes these people to want to hurt back usually not caring who it is. In a strange way they think they are evening the score. Some have never learned to control themselves but they want to control you and believe you "owe" them your allegiance.

People who act like bullies want to feel powerful so badly they don't play fair. They may tease or bait you by calling you names or calling someone you care about names. They might accuse you of being (scared, dumb, ugly, chicken, a dork, whatever) or take something from you but only when they have the advantage like when they are in a group or if they have a weapon. These people hit below the belt any way they can to sucker you into a fight. They do it to get a power high.

Obviously, rule #1 is to stay as far away from people who act like this as you can. Life can be very tough for individuals who have people like this in their lives, however. Maybe one of your parents has this kind of boss, or one of your siblings has one on his or her sports team. Worst of all is having a person who behaves this way as a member of the family.

When an episode occurs and the deck is stacked against you, what can you do to end it without becoming a victim and without grovelling? This is a time to breathe deeply, control yourself, and remember the anger and conflict management strategies you have learned.

Here are some specific suggestions:

- First and foremost: Don't take the bait! This means don't argue, trade insults, or try to seriously reason with a person who is acting like a bully.
- Gaze calmly at the person. Keep a tall posture and above all, don't show fear. If the person demands you give him or her your money or something else, hold your dignity and say something like: "Aw come on, (Jack). You're no thief."
- Agree. Imagine the person has just called you stupid. Your response, perhaps with a smile: "Yep. You may be right. But I do my best." Then walk away, keeping eye contact.
- Give them what they want. If more than one of them grabs one of your belongings and throws it back and forth baiting you to try to get it, don't. Just say, "If you like it so much, you can have it." This ends the game and they are likely to throw the item where you can get it later. If it's outright theft, let your property go. Report the theft to the authorities if and when you think it's safe.
- Don't physically fight anyone acting like a bully, unless you have been physically attacked and you have to defend yourself. Unfortunately, this is the only language some of these people understand.

- When you aren't being threatened you might want to try showing genuine civil respect and kindness to these people. (Doing this doesn't mean you will allow yourself to come under their control.) Psychologists tell us that it's the most unlovable person who needs love the most.

Think about a time you were bullied that you would be comfortable sharing with your team members. Without mentioning names tell them what happened, how you felt at the time and what you did.

Write a brief description of the incident you told your team members about here:

_____

_____

_____

_____

Pass this experience sheet to the other members of your team for their ideas for how you might have responded to the person you told about. (Do the same for them on their experience sheets.)

Here's a space for team members to write down their ideas for ways to respond to the person you described:

_____

_____

_____

_____

_____

_____
_____
_____
_____
_____
_____
_____
_____
_____

Let's review...

- No one is born a bully; their actions have become a set of learned destructive behaviors and habits.
- People who behave like bullies try to fool others and themselves into thinking they are strong when, in fact, their behavior is a cover up for inner feelings of weakness and vulnerability.
- Bullying behaviors come from the urge to hurt others because these people have been hurt or imagine they have been hurt. They believe that hurting others is a way to settle the score.
- Many of these people believe the world is out to get them making it their right to get what they want however they can.
- These people and their victims need genuine caring and kindness.
- Self-control and anger management skills are helpful in dealing with people who bully others and for them in dealing with themselves.

Lesson 20: Check Your Memory!

Purpose:

This summary learning activity helps students refocus on some of the key concepts and skills presented in each of the lessons on self control and anger management in this curriculum beginning with Lesson #1.

Materials:

A copy of the Student Experience Sheet #20, *"Check Your Memory!"* for each student

Directions:

1. **Begin by acknowledging the students for their willing participation**! Point out: *"You have been great participants in all of the lessons we've experienced together about how to control ourselves and manage our anger. You've leaned many new concepts, pointers and skills. You can take pride in the personal power you have gained!"*

2. **Direct the students to form teams of four.** Explain: *"All of the combined lessons we have been focusing on together have provided lots of ideas and skills to help us control ourselves and manage our anger in order to become more personally powerful. In this last lesson we will revisit some of those ideas and skills."*

3. **Distribute Student Experience Sheet #20, *"Check Your Memory."*** Explain: *"This final experience sheet lists some of the statements in the "Did you know ...?" and the "Let's review ..." segments in the experience sheets. As you can see the statements are listed under the lesson titles.*

   "The first statement for each lesson has one or two words missing. (If there are two blanks in a statement it's because it's the same word.) Read the statements over and discuss them with your team. See how many of the blanks you can fill in together without going to any of the experience sheets you've already filled in. Each of you should write in the words on your own experience sheet #20.

   "The second statement for each lesson is either true or false. Circle the T for statements you believe are true. Circle the F for statements you believe are false.

"This is not to be graded. It's a review and a summary of the many things you have learned about self control and anger management. You will have _____ minutes. See if you can get to all of the statements. Go!"

4. **Make this "revisitation" enjoyable!** Be on hand to help the students if they become confused by some of the wordings and need clarification. Be aware that as they try different words to fill in the blanks some of them will sound hilarious and normal laughter is bound to occur. Enjoy the process with them. It's a positive way for everyone to reduce tension.

5. **Initiate team reports to confirm correct answers.** When the students have completed filling in all of the blanks, call on a team member from one team to read the statements from Lesson 1 and how his/her team responded to them. As necessary, use your key, below, to clarify correct responses. Next, call on a team member on another team to do the same for the statements from Lesson 2. Continue in this manner until all of the statements from all 19 lessons have been read and correct responses have been clarified.

Note: Synonyms, such as "actions" and "behavior," are both correct responses to the fill-in-the-blank statements.

6. **Direct the students to select those statements with the most personal impact.** Explain: *"You've absorbed a lot of concepts from these lessons that foster self control and anger management. Now, please scan them and decide which ideas or concepts were especially important for you. Maybe it was an idea that opened your eyes to a new way of looking at something. It could have been a concept that confirmed something you were already working on in your mind. Perhaps it was something that inspired you to develop more personal power. Pick the ones that were the most meaningful for you personally by drawing a star beside each one. Select about five. After you have completed doing that you'll have a chance to talk about one or two with your team members. Any questions?"*

7. **Initiate team sharing about the students' most important statements.** Explain: *"As soon as all of your team members have placed the stars beside the statements that are especially meaningful, begin taking turns telling each other why they are important."*

8. **Close by directing the student's attention to the statements that appear at the end of the experience sheet after the questions on Lesson 19.** Read them together. Give the students your personal thanks for their participation and contributions. Encourage them to keep their experience sheets as a resource whenever life hands them a self control or anger management issue as it surely will.

KEY: The statements from each lesson with the blanks <u>filled in</u> as well as the answers to the true/false items with clarifying statements are shown here:

Lesson 1: It's Just a Feeling!

Anger is simply one of many normal human emotions, and as such, is neither good nor bad in a moral sense. (It's just a <u>feeling</u>.)

Everyone has the right to feel <u>anger</u> when provoked. *"True. Feeling anger does not make you a bad person. It's what you do with your anger that matters."*

Lesson 2: What's Under that Volcano?

<u>Self</u>-honesty is the first step in anger management. It allows you to avoid being a victim and to make good conscious choices about what to do.

Facing into your own anger is always easy. *"False. Sometimes it is very hard because we would rather avoid facing the discomfort."*

Lesson 3: You Be the Judge!

Anger often occurs after deeper, primary emotions are being felt. This kind of anger is often "blind," impulsively spurring <u>behavior</u> that is destructive to yourself and others.

Instead of taking impulsive, destructive actions in provoking situations, it is possible to use judgement and decide to act in alternate ways that are constructive, or at least neutral. *"True. The key word is <u>decide</u>."*

Lesson 4: What about the Consequences?

Impulsive actions taken without using good judgement and self-control can lead to unpleasant and unrewarding <u>consequences</u> not only for you *but others too.*

It is smart to consider the consequences of an action before doing it especially when you are angry. *"True. Calm down, decide what to do that won't get anyone hurt, including you. Then do it."*

Lesson 5: Look at It Another Way

We interpret our <u>perceptions</u> into thoughts like conclusions and judgements, which in turn spur feelings and actions.

Sometimes our interpretations of perceptions lead to incorrect conclusions and judgements as well as inappropriate—even damaging--emotions and actions. *"True. It's best to ask ourselves if we're 'seeing' things correctly. It often helps to look at situations another way before taking action."*

Lesson 6: How Do You Talk to Yourself?

Self-talk can be helpful and encouraging or hurtful and damaging.

Self-talk cannot be controlled or guided. *"False. You can control and guide what you say to yourself. If you will, you can calm yourself and think carefully about what's going on and what to do. That's when you have personal power!"*

Lesson 7: Avoid these four traps!

Four mental and emotional traps (Past and Present Mixups, Gunnysacking, Acting on Habit and Having Unrealistic Expectations) make it hard for people to make good choices, stay in control of themselves, and manage their anger. Each one usually leads to unpleasant consequences.

Past and present mixups happen when exactly the very same thing that happened before is happening again. *"False. Past and present mixups happen when people think the same painful past event is happening again causing them the same painful upset as before. In truth no two events are exactly the same—only similar."*

Lesson 8: Four More Traps to Avoid!

Four more mental and emotional traps (Unconscious Imitation, Displacement, Rationalization and Acting Out) make it hard for people to make good choices, stay in control of themselves, and manage their anger. These also usually lead to unpleasant consequences.

When you are angry, Acting Out is a way to put your drama skills to work that others will admire. *"False. When you are acting out you are out-of-control and people will generally not admire your behavior."*

Lesson 9: Grudges are Poison

A grievance turns into a grudge if you are giving lots of your mental time and energy to it. You are also "swallowing" poison if you keep thinking negative thoughts about it without trying to resolve or solve it in some way.

When you hold a grudge against someone you are giving them control over you by allowing them to occupy your mind. *"True. Think of it this way: you are letting them live inside your head rent-free!"*

Lesson 10: Revenge Is Not Sweet for Long!

Revenge often results from holding a grudge.

When wronged, the urge to "get even" may be strong, but the act of taking revenge frequently backfires. *"True. Getting even often leads to more attacks. Both sides suffer until or unless the problem is resolved in a way both can accept."*

Lesson 11: Start Out Fresh!

Sometimes anger turned inward is a poisonous grudge we hold against ourselves for mistakes we have made.

You should feel guilty and punish yourself for mistakes you made in the past. *"False. Mistakes are best seen as errors that we can decide not to repeat; often these errors can be corrected with helpful actions. Use mistakes as teachers. Punishing yourself with guilt is not useful."*

Lesson 12: Use Your Anger—Don't Let It Use *You!*

Using anger, instead of letting it use you, is one of the highest expressions of self-control and anger management! It's a great way to build personal power!

It is not possible to use the energy your anger gives you to your advantage. *"False. Angry energy can be used to get you to do something necessary you might not do otherwise."*

Lesson 13: You've Got the Power!

Using your mind to visualize positive outcomes in difficult situations helps you manage your anger and make those outcomes happen.

Deep breathing weakens your power of self-control in difficult situations. *"False. Deep breathing is a powerful strategy you can use anytime to calm yourself and think straight."*

Lesson 14: Be Assertive!

The aggressive and submissive styles of behavior with others come from feelings of inner weakness; the assertive style comes from inner feelings of confidence and strength.

The reward for assertive self-talk and action is positive personal power! *"True. When you consciously behave assertively you will feel in control and know you are experiencing positive personal power!"*

Lesson 15: Stand Up For Yourself!

Sometimes it's necessary to confront people for their offensive actions. How you confront them could be constructive or destructive.

The use of an "I Message" is an aggressive way to confront a person when it's necessary. *"False. Using an "I Message" is an assertive and constructive way to confront someone when necessary."*

Lesson 16: Assertive Conflict Management Strategies that Work!

Conflicts arise in all of our lives. When they do we can respond in <u>aggressive</u>, submissive or assertive ways.

Self control to remain <u>silent</u> and patient until a person who is upset finishes talking is the key to the strategy, "Listen to Understand." *"True. This can be difficult but it may likely lead to a positive outcome. Keep in mind that you are using self control to everyone's advantage when you are able to use this strategy."*

Lesson 17: More Assertive Conflict Management Strategies that Work

Self control to determine that conditions are not good for trying to resolve a conflict *right now* is the key to the strategy, <u>postponing</u>.

Blaming others is the key to problem solving. *"False. Understanding how unhelpful it is to blame another person for a problem is the first key to successful problem solving."*

Lesson 18: Don't Cave to the Pressure!

People who pressure you to do something that could get you in trouble do it because they don't want to be all by <u>themselves</u>.

People who pressure you in this way generally don't care about your health and safety. *"True. They are taking advantage of you."*

Lesson 19: How to Respond to Bullying Behavior

People who are acting like bullies try to fool others and *themselves* into thinking they are strong when, in fact, their behavior is a cover up for inner feelings of weakness and vulnerability.

Many people who act like bullies believe the world is out to get them making it their right to get what they want however they can. *"True. Many of these people have the urge to hurt others because they have been hurt or imagine they have been hurt. They believe that hurting others is a way to settle the score. Self-control and anger management skills are helpful in dealing with them and for them in dealing with themselves."*

Check Your Memory!

Student Experience Sheet #20

Congratulations! You have learned dozens of ideas and concepts for controlling yourself and managing your anger from the 19 lessons in this curriculum. This lesson, #20, is a chance for you to revisit some of those ideas and concepts to see how well you remember them.

Look at the statements below. There are two for each of the 19 lessons. A key word or words have been changed to blanks in the first statement for each lesson. (If there are two blanks it's because it's the same word.) See how many blanks you can fill in!

The second statement for each lesson is either true or false. Circle the T if you think it is true. Circle the F if you think it is false. See how many you can get right!

As you fill in the blanks keep an eye open for the statements that mean the most to you personally. Later, you may be given a chance to tell your team why one or two are especially meaningful to you.

Lesson 1: It's Just a Feeling!

Anger is simply one of many normal human emotions, and as such, is neither good nor bad in a moral sense. (It's just a _____.)

T/F: Everyone has the right to feel anger when provoked.

Lesson 2: What's Under that Volcano?

_____-honesty is the first step in anger management. It allows you to avoid being a victim and to make good conscious choices about what to do.

T/F: Facing into your own feelings of anger is always easy.

149

Lesson 3: You Be the Judge!

Anger often occurs after deeper, primary emotions are being felt. This kind of anger is often "blind," impulsively spurring _____ that is destructive to yourself and others.

T/F: Instead of taking impulsive, destructive actions in provoking situations, it is possible to use judgement and decide to act in alternate ways that are constructive, or at least neutral.

Lesson 4: What about the Consequences?

Impulsive actions taken without using good judgement and self-control can lead to unpleasant and unrewarding _____ not only for you *but others too*.

T/F: It is smart to consider the consequences of an action before doing it especially when you are angry.

Lesson 5: Look at It Another Way

We interpret our _____ into thoughts like conclusions and judgements, which in turn spur feelings and actions.

T/F: Sometimes our interpretations of perceptions lead to incorrect conclusions and judgements as well as inappropriate—even damaging--emotions and actions.

Lesson 6: How Do You Talk to Yourself?

Self-talk can be _____ and encouraging or hurtful and damaging.

T/F: Self-talk cannot be controlled or guided.

Lesson 7: Avoid these four traps!

Four mental and emotional traps (Past and Present Mixups, Gunnysacking, Acting on Habit and Having Unrealistic Expectations) make it hard for people to make good _____, stay in control of themselves, and manage their anger. Each one usually leads to unpleasant consequences.

T/F: Past and present mixups happen when exactly the very same thing that happened before is happening again.

Lesson 8: Four More Traps to Avoid!

Four more mental and emotional traps (Unconscious Imitation, Displacement, Rationalization and Acting Out) make it hard for people to make good choices, stay in _____ of themselves, and manage their anger. These also usually lead to unpleasant consequences.

T/F: When you are angry, Acting Out is a way to put your drama skills to work that others will admire.

Lesson 9: Grudges are Poison

A grievance turns into a _____ if you are giving lots of your mental time and energy to it. You are also "swallowing" poison if you keep thinking negative thoughts about it without trying to resolve or solve it in some way.

T/F: When you hold a grudge against someone you are giving them power over you by allowing them to occupy your mind.

Lesson 10: Revenge Is Not Sweet for Long!

Revenge often results from holding a _____.

T/F: When wronged, the urge to "get even" may be strong, but the act of taking revenge frequently backfires.

Lesson 11: Start Out Fresh!

Sometimes anger turned inward is a poisonous grudge we hold against _____ for mistakes we have made.

T/F: You should feel guilty and punish yourself for mistakes you made in the past.

Lesson 12: Use Your Anger—Don't Let It Use *You!*

Using anger, instead of letting it use _____, is one of the highest expressions of self-control and anger management! It's a great way to build personal power!

T/F: It is not possible to use the energy your anger gives you to your advantage.

Lesson 13: You've Got the Power!

Using your mind to visualize _____ outcomes in difficult situations helps you manage your anger and make those positive outcomes happen.

T/F: Deep breathing weakens your power of self-control in difficult situations.

Lesson 14: Be Assertive!

The aggressive and submissive styles of behavior with others come from _____ of inner weakness; the assertive style comes from inner _____ of confidence and strength.

T/F: The reward for assertive self-talk and action is positive personal power!

Lesson 15: Stand Up For Yourself!

Sometimes it's necessary to confront people for their offensive actions. How you confront them could be _____ or destructive.

T/F: The use of an "I Message" is an aggressive way to confront someone when it's necessary.

Lesson 16: Assertive Conflict Management Strategies that Work!

Conflicts arise in all of our lives. When they do we can respond in _____, submissive or assertive ways.

T/F: Self control to remain silent and patient until a person who is upset finishes talking is the key to using the strategy, "Listen to Understand."

Lesson 17: More Assertive Conflict Management Strategies that Work

Self control to determine that conditions are not good for trying to resolve a conflict right now is the key to the strategy, _____.

T/F: Blaming others is the key to problem solving.

Lesson 18: Don't Cave to the Pressure!

People who pressure you to do something that could get you in trouble do it because they don't want to be all by _____.

T/F: People who pressure you in this way generally don't care about your health and safety.

Lesson 19: How to Respond to Bullying Behavior

People who are acting like bullies try to fool others and _____ into thinking they are strong when, in fact, their behavior is a cover up for inner feelings of weakness and vulnerability.

T/F: Many people who act like bullies believe the world is out to get them making it their right to get what they want however they can.

These lessons to help you develop self control and anger management skills are basic training for life! Keep your experience sheets and your memories of what you've learned to help you prepare for the "classroom of the world" and all its challenges. *That class is always in session!*

Stay in touch with your personal power and how to use it!

**If your heart is in
Social-Emotional Learning,
visit us online**

Come see us at
www.InnerchoicePublishing.com

Our web site gives you a look at all our other
Social-Emotional Learning-based books, free activities,
articles, research, and learning and teaching strategies.

Subscribe to our weekly blog, and every week you'll receive
a new activity or Sharing Circle topic and lesson.

INNERCHOICE Publishing
15079 Oak Chase Court
Wellington, FL 33414

www.InnerchoicePublishing.com

www.ingramcontent.com/pod-product-compliance
Lightning Source LLC
Chambersburg PA
CBHW081217230426
43666CB00015B/2771